# THE SOUTHWEST PACIFIC AND THE WAR

# THE SOUTHWEST PACIFIC AND THE WAR

LECTURES DELIVERED UNDER THE AUSPICES OF THE
COMMITTEE ON INTERNATIONAL RELATIONS
ON THE LOS ANGELES CAMPUS OF THE
UNIVERSITY OF CALIFORNIA
SPRING 1943

GREENWOOD PRESS, PUBLISHERS
WESTPORT, CONNECTICUT

**Library of Congress Cataloging in Publication Data**

California. University. University at Los Angeles.
  Committee on International Relations.
    The Southwest Pacific and the war.

  Reprint of the 1944 ed. published by University of
California Press, Berkeley.
  Bibliography: p.
  CONTENTS: Zierer, C. M. The geographic background.
--Hoijer, H. Peoples and cultures of the Southwest
Pacific.--Mowat, C. L. The entry of the Southwest
Pacific into world politics. [etc.]
  1. World War, 1939-1945--Oceanica--Addresses,
essays, lectures.  2.  Oceanica--Description and travel
--Addresses, essays, lectures.  3.  Ethnology--Oceanica
--Addresses, essays, lectures.   I.  Title.
D767.9.C34  1974       940.53'9       74-3750
ISBN 0-8371-7473-2

COPYRIGHT, 1944, BY
THE REGENTS OF THE UNIVERSITY OF CALIFORNIA

Originally published in 1944 by the University of
California Press, Berkeley and Los Angeles

Reprinted from an original copy in the collections of
the University of Illinois Library

Reprinted in 1974 by Greenwood Press,
a division of Williamhouse-Regency Inc.

Library of Congress Catalog Card Number 74-3750

ISBN 0-8371-7473-2

Printed in the United States of America

# PREFACE

It is now some thirty years since the University of California was asked by the Directors of the Panama-Pacific International Exposition to assume a major responsibility for guiding the thinking of the great historical and other congresses which were to assemble in San Francisco to commemorate and celebrate the completion of the Panama Canal. The University was quick to respond and suggested as the theme of a number of scientific gatherings the role of the Pacific Ocean in history. The unforgettable Henry Morse Stephens, historian of the British Empire in its far-flung extent, voiced his *credo* for the age that was even then being born and suffering all the pains of childbirth: the history of the Ancient World was centered on the Mediterranean; that of the Middle Ages on the Baltic; that of the Modern World has been the history of the Atlantic Basin; the history of the future lies in the Pacific Basin. This was strange utterance, particularly coming from the lips of an Englishman. And yet, as the years have passed, the verdict of history has not failed to corroborate what, save for the reverence in which he was held by his contemporaries, seemed, even in Henry Morse Stephens, heretical doctrine. The curt, terse, adage which the first San Francisco World's Fair emblazoned on its escutcheon, "The Land Divided, the World United," has indeed been borne out in history, but in far less pacific ways than its progenitors could have imagined. The physical land was indeed divided at Gatun, at Pedro Miguel, at Miraflores; but the thing which has united the world in our day is not its commerce merely, but its faith in the larger destiny of mankind as it shifts its principal habitat from the Atlantic that has been its center for half a millennium to the Pacific that has been its focal point for half a century.

In the vast conflict in which we are engaged, the thing that stands stronger than any Confederacy of Commerce is a Confederation of Faith—an active union of the nations bordering the Pacific area in quest of a military victory which will make possible the peaceful symbiosis, around the theater that is the Pacific, of free men. Save for one arrogant, criminal power on the Pacific, there is no question of the community of interest that unites the peoples of this vast basin—a community of interest that is more than an animal struggle for survival, that is the quest for the terms of association which can make a tolerable life possible to men of good will. In this common quest we of America and Mexico and Canada, along with the other American Republics bordering on the Pacific, are at one with the great forces of Russia and China, struggling but undefeated, and of Korea, the Philippines, and Insulinde, defeated but still struggling for their elemental birthright of freedom.

More poignant in its immediate, as well as its ultimate, significance and outcome is the war to the two peoples "down under," the million and a half inhabitants of New Zealand, and the seven million that make up Australia. They are the real touchstones to capacity for survival in the Pacific area, for if they cannot maintain their free status after this war, and as a result of the terms on which this conflict is ended, the lights will go out in a very large part of the world. It is the consciousness of that possibility that stands out primordially in the utterances and pronouncements of virtually every man in public life in Australia or New Zealand. For never before in the life of the Australasian peoples has so fundamental an issue been raised. That is why it becomes almost tragically necessary for Australia and New Zealand to become ruthlessly articulate, stridently adamant in their insistence on the maintenance of their independence. And yet, when I say "independence" I do not use the word in its strictly traditional, nineteenth-century sense. The people of Australasia are now learning, as the people of Indonesia learned to their sorrow and too late, that independence is not to be thought of solely in terms of a mother country, but of the prime factors operating in the circumjacent world—in this case, overwhelmingly, Japan.

The emergence of the two "Pacific Dominions," as Professor Condliffe calls them, from their own "splendid isolation" of a particularly parochial variety in the past to the center-stage position they now occupy on the world scene, has moved, across the span of half a century, *pari passu* with the advances of the Empire of the Rising Sun. But for the shaking off of the shackles of extraterritoriality by Japan after 1895, the otherwise purely "domestic," "constitutional" question of securing dominion status and federal union quite simultaneously could have waited longer—it had already taken half a century to approach discussion—in Australia. But for the successes of Nipponese arms in the Russo-Japanese War in 1905, it is equally likely that the matter of dominion status for New Zealand, already rejected as an adjunct to Australian federation, could have waited indefinitely. As late as 1897, at the time of the Second Imperial Conference, both Australia and New Zealand were considered to be strictly colonial territory; by 1911, they, along with South Africa, enjoyed dominion status, then a term of ill-defined content but basically held to be constitutional only.

A clearly discernible third stage in the evolution of the Pacific Dominions came with World War I when the Anzacs earned, in the sweat, blood, and tears of Gallipoli, the international recognition of their achieved coördinate military status with other allies. By joint participation in the Imperial Conferences of wartime, by joint representation at the Peace Conference, by membership coördinate with that of Britain in the reorganized Society of Nations, the Dominions "down under" achieved not only their "baptism of fire," but their final formal accolade in entering the general Community of Nations.

In the retrospect of twenty-four years, the stern insistence of Australia and New Zealand on an unfettered right to control their newly won positions in Samoa and New Guinea after World War I seems far more to have been horse sense than the petty, bickering, chauvinist nationalism which it was painted to the Western World. Not only London, but Washington, Canberra, and Auckland, must rue the day when, with their free or reluctant consent, the flag of the Rising Sun was raised over the Japanese mandated islands in the Pacific. Australasian nationalism was beaten in an hour of maudlin sentimental internationalism of a peculiarly insidious sort, but it was made more articulate, more vociferous in consequence, not only at home but abroad.

In the two decades between wars, Australia and New Zealand emerged from their previously confining juridical chrysalises to find a new field of fine, level-headed, coöperative activity, first in the British Commonwealth, where ties of association and loyalty blended with those of interest and convenience, and second at Geneva, where their influence rose steadily and was impartially exercised. Finally, in the naval and arms-limitation conferences of unhappy memory, they came in contact with the United States and Japan and laid their foundations for the eventual establishment of separate, that is, "independent," diplomatic services—curiously designed to link them to the United States on the one hand, and to permit detailed observation of Japan on the other. This genuinely significant fourth phase may be noted as amazingly coincident with the renewal of Japanese aggressions on the Asiatic continent. It ended on December 7, 1941, so far as Japan was concerned; in a sense, it continues now toward the United States; in yet another sense, it becomes blended with the events of the war itself, which bring the Dominions "down under" into a clear-cut fifth stage: that of United Nations activity in the Southwest Pacific. Here the role of Australia and New Zealand rises to an all-time high of military and political significance.

One is led, by the very impacts of the war, to speculate on the future of these two dominions. Should the war be lost in the Pacific—a contingency happily remote but not out of the range of probability,—we will not need to know what fate has in store for them: their fate is writ large in Malaysia and the Philippines. In the event of victory, it is obvious that the new-found relationship to the United States will play a role as great as that which has been traditionally theirs in the British Commonwealth of Nations.

MALBONE W. GRAHAM

# CONTENTS

|  | PAGE |
|---|---|
| *The Geographic Background* . . . . . . . . . . . . | 3 |
| By CLIFFORD M. ZIERER, Associate Professor of Geography | |
| *Peoples and Cultures of the Southwest Pacific* . . . . | 31 |
| By HARRY HOIJER, Assistant Professor of Anthropology | |
| *The Entry of the Southwest Pacific into World Politics* . | 71 |
| By CHARLES L. MOWAT, Assistant Professor of History | |
| *The Pacific in the Diplomatic Conflict of the War* . . . | 105 |
| By ROBERT J. KERNER, Sather Professor of History | |
| *Strategy* . . . . . . . . . . . . . . . . . . | 131 |
| By WILLIAM C. BARKER, Professor of Naval Science and Tactics | |
| *The Pacific Dominions* . . . . . . . . . . . . | 155 |
| By J. B. CONDLIFFE, Professor of Economics | |

# THE GEOGRAPHIC BACKGROUND

---

CLIFFORD M. ZIERER

ASSOCIATE PROFESSOR OF GEOGRAPHY
IN THE UNIVERSITY OF CALIFORNIA

*Lecture delivered March 29, 1943*

# THE GEOGRAPHIC BACKGROUND

THE PACIFIC BASIN comprises the most extensive battleground over which man has ever fought. The arena of the Pacific war covers nearly half the surface of the earth. From Panama on the east to Singapore on the west it is 11,800 miles. From Alaska in the north to New Zealand in the south, a distance of more than 7,500 miles must be taken into account. The Pacific Ocean covers a larger portion of the earth's surface than all the continents taken together. It is almost twice the size of the Atlantic and three times the size of the Indian Ocean. The Pacific is the largest physical unit on the face of the earth.[1]

The vast distances which separate our centers of production from the fighting fronts slow down our offensive action against Japan. The battle of the Pacific will have to be in large measure won along the supply routes. Convoys are able to make relatively few round trips in the course of a year; thus large numbers of ships are required to deliver a steady stream of men and supplies to the fighting fronts. Only by means of enormous shipping facilities will it be possible to carry the war to the Japanese, and that is the only way in which the war can be won.

Long-range bombers and cargo planes are playing an important part in overcoming the immense distances involved in the Pacific theater of war. It is only with the most modern means of transport that military campaigns can be effectively conducted over such a far-flung region. The great size of the Pacific requires a strategy for war greatly different from that which may be successful in more limited areas of conflict.

Although great distances handicap our prosecution of the war in numerous ways, the great width of the Pacific also serves as an element of protection for home shores against enemy attack. Thus our superior productive capacity will in due course be reflected on the fighting fronts by an avalanche of the implements of war.

[1] Felix Riesenberg, *The Pacific Ocean* (New York, 1940).

The conflict in the Pacific has been described in its earlier stages as a "race for bases." Hawaii is America's most powerful Pacific base and the pivot of our naval line of defense and offense. Midway, Johnston, and Palmyra form the first screen of defense for Pearl Harbor. An outer screen is composed of Wake (now in Japanese hands), Howland, Baker, Canton, Jarvis, and other tiny islets. Guam lies well along the way to Manila but is in the midst of the Japanese Mandate. Aleutian Islands bases are highly significant in the northern reaches of the Pacific, and Samoa lies along the route to New Zealand and Australia.[2]

The United States has essentially complete control of all significant bases in the eastern Pacific, thus making effective attack upon the shores of the Americas especially difficult. The relative scarcity of islands in the eastern portion of the Pacific, useful as bases for attack upon the Americas, might be claimed as a geographic advantage to the nations of the Western Hemisphere.

The United States also enjoys the use of other bases belonging to friendly powers, especially in the southwest quarter of the Pacific. Many British and French bases are now available to us and Dutch bases will become available later. Most important of the Allied Nations' bases in the southwest Pacific are Australia and New Zealand. Australia is a base of continental proportions and is capable of serving either as a bastion for defense or as a springboard for offensive action of major proportions.[3]

Japan, likewise, has its island outposts for defense or offense. The Kurile chain extends northeasterly in the direction of Kamchatka, and the Bonin and Marianas Islands form connecting links with the widely spaced atolls of the Caroline and Marshall groups lying squarely astride the American supply route to the Philippines. By early offensive action Japan secured innumerable other bases on the Asiatic mainland, throughout the Netherlands Indies, and in New

[2] A. R. Elliott, "United States Outposts in the Pacific," *Foreign Policy Report*, March 15, 1941.
[3] Charles J. Rolo and Alwyn Lee, "Australia: Bastion and Springboard," *Harper's Magazine*, Vol. 184 (April, 1942), pp. 509–514.

Guinea, the Solomons, the Gilberts, and elsewhere. Attacks upon the Aleutian Islands and Hawaii, farther removed from strong home bases, were less successful. Japan, however, controls the northwest quarter of the Pacific and she has effectively breached the convenient trade routes through the Indies. It now appears that Japan will attempt to hold her outer ring of bases while she hastily exploits her recently acquired territories and resources. Sooner or later the Allied Nations will need to break through the encircling defenses and establish strong operating bases within effective military range of the Japanese industrial and military centers. The successful completion of such operations would place many of the widely scattered Japanese forces "out on a limb" and island-by-island conquest would not be requisite to an Allied victory. With naval and aerial operations likely to be the determining phases of military activities in the Pacific theater, the importance of strategic bases cannot be overemphasized.

In the first round of the war, Japan was highly successful in grabbing strategic bases from which attacks might have been made upon her homeland as well as upon her recently acquired realm. Some of those bases will have to be recovered as the Allied strategy of war unfolds.

Up to the present time the southwest Pacific has been the most active theater of operations in the conflict between Allied and Japanese forces. The conquest of southeast Asia and the Netherlands Indies was quickly accomplished by the Japanese, and even Australia and India were endangered. Effective resistance, however, was marshaled by the Allied Nations in the latter areas and Japanese expansion was checked. Subsequent action has been centered chiefly in the New Guinea–Solomons area adjacent to the supply lines between the United States and Australia. Future events may shift the main theater of operations to some other part of the Pacific.

Before the outbreak of war with Japan most Americans had only slight acquaintance with the lands of the southwest Pacific. The dispatch of troops to many places in that section of the globe and numerous military engagements among the island groups have now created an intense interest in the geography of that portion of the world. Australia, New Guinea, the Solomons, and New Britain have suddenly become household words throughout the length and breadth of America. A widespread interest has been created in the kinds of people inhabiting those lands and in the way they make their living. Information about the conditions of climate, vegetation, topography, and coastlines is sought by many in order to gain a better understanding of the events of the day. The geographic conditions furnish the background not only for the conduct of peaceful pursuits, but also for the general plan and the conduct of war. The future relationships between those people and Americans are becoming matters of concern to many of our citizens.

Australia has an area approximately equal to that of the continental United States. The population, however, is only seven millions or about one-twentieth that of our own. There is little likelihood that its population will ever become greater than fifteen or twenty millions (if present standards of living are maintained), because of the large proportion of arid and semiarid lands. While America has a fertile and well-watered agricultural interior supporting great cities and industries, the heart of Australia is at best a region of scattered pastoral and mining activities. After more than a hundred and fifty years of occupation most of the interior as well as the north coast region has not even one person per square mile. Most Australians live in a comparatively narrow belt along the southeast coast between Brisbane and Adelaide and in the far southwest corner near Perth. In those coastal districts rainfall is more abundant and living conditions are especially attractive. Tropical temperatures, the marked seasonality of rainfall, and poor soils have combined to prevent successful development of the extensive north coast region.

Nearly two-thirds of all Australians reside in cities and towns, thus making that Commonwealth relatively more urbanized than even the United States. Half the entire population lives in the six capital cities. One-third of all Australians live in Sydney and Melbourne alone, the two outstanding metropolitan centers. The preponderance of urban population is related especially to the traditional British urban background, to the large-scale and mechanized character of agricultural industries, and to the growing importance of manufacturing. The most characteristic Australian is a city dweller rather than a farmer or a pastoralist.

Although more than 95 per cent of the Australians are of British extraction, no fewer than 86 per cent were born in Australia and 10 per cent in Great Britain. They are ardent in their feelings toward Australia but they are also devoted members of the British Commonwealth of Nations. Other Europeans (including Italians, Germans, Greeks, Russians, and French), along with Asiatics (principally Chinese), comprise the minor population groups. Although there are about sixty thousand aboriginals remaining in Australia, most of them live in the little-developed central and northern districts and have slight contact with the white population. The "white Australia policy" has prevented the immigration of colored races in recent decades.

Life in Australia resembles very closely that which is characteristic of the southwestern United States. Sydney and Melbourne are not very different from Los Angeles and San Francisco. Its smaller inland towns resemble in many ways the agricultural and mining centers of California, Utah, Arizona, and Nevada. Landscapes in New Mexico and in western Texas and Oklahoma frequently suggest Australian scenes.

Sheepmen, cattlemen, wheat farmers, dairymen, and specialists in irrigated fruit growing are most numerous among the rural population. Sheep stations (ranches) including many square miles of grassland and thousands of merinos are the most characteristic type of settlement unit. Highly mechanized wheat growing on large acreages is done on the western slopes of the eastern uplands and elsewhere along the southern margins of the continent. Cattle raising is important in many favorable districts in the interior and in places along the north coast. Smaller holdings cleared of forest growth and planted to introduced grasses are typical of the dairy farms along the moist eastern coastal region.

Irrigation communities, closely resembling those of California and other western states, are associated with the Murray River and its larger tributaries. The citrus groves with their packing sheds could have been lifted out of the southern California scene. Vineyards, deciduous fruit and nut orchards, alfalfa fields, and irrigation ditches remind the visitor of landscapes in many parts of our own Southwest. Sugar-cane farms provide the principal basis for settlement in the eastern coastal district of Queensland. The production of tropical fruits and mining provide a livelihood for additional numbers of persons in tropical Queensland.

Mining has long been an important phase of economic activity in Australia. The gold rushes, similar to those in California, attracted many settlers to Victoria during the 1850's and to western Australia during the late 1880's and early 1890's. During the middle 1930's gold was the most valuable mineral produced in Australia, as also during many years prior to 1900. Australia is comparatively rich in lead and zinc, with Broken Hill, in the arid interior, as the chief center of production.[4] Coal is the most important mineral resource in Australia not only because it normally exceeds gold in value of output, but also because it serves as the principal source of power for transport and industry. Australia is lacking in natural petroleum, and water power is limited because of the widespread scanty rainfall.

Urban life in Australia is as varied as it is in America.[5] All types of industry, merchandising, transportation, and recreation are available. At one time Australia was engaged principally in the production of raw materials for export, depending on England for most kinds of manufactured goods in return. Now Australian factories

---

[4] Clifford M. Zierer, "Broken Hill: Australia's Greatest Mining Camp," *Annals of the Association of American Geographers,* Vol. 30 (June, 1940), pp. 83–108.

[5] Clifford M. Zierer, "Melbourne as a Functional Center," *Annals of the Association of American Geographers,* Vol. 31 (December, 1941), pp. 251–288, "Land Use Differentiation in Sydney, Australia," *ibid.,* Vol. 32 (September, 1942), pp. 255–308, and "Brisbane—River Metropolis of Queensland," *Economic Geography,* Vol. 17 (October, 1941), pp. 325–344.

produce a sufficient variety of nearly all kinds of manufactures to meet home needs, with a surplus of some things for export. Even complete airplanes, tanks, and warships are being manufactured in Australia to serve on the fighting fronts.

During recent years the Commonwealth has developed a substantial production of the tools of war with the investment of large amounts of new capital and the training and employment of large numbers of new industrial workers. An important steel industry with the usual array of accessory industries has been developed, based upon local iron and coal resources and certain important alloy metals.[6] Bauxite deposits occur there and aluminum alloys are being produced for use in airplane manufacture. The large state railway shops have been converted to produce parts for aircraft, tanks, and gun carriages. Australia has gone far in gearing its industrial and human resources for war.[7]

The great importance of Australia in the production of foodstuffs and its growing importance in manufacturing have been favorable factors in establishing a major base for military operations there by the Allied Nations.

Important elements in the Australian landscape are the many types of native eucalyptus trees, some varieties of which are now widely planted in California. They range in kind from the giant timber trees of the moist southeast and southwest districts to the small, brilliantly flowered varieties of the western state. Typical of the interior semiarid plains is the acacia (or mulga), which provides great masses of golden bloom as well as feed for sheep in times of severe drought. Tree-dotted grasslands provide excellent pasturage for sheep and cattle over wide areas near the headwaters of the Murray River and its tributaries. Desert scrub, with some useful forage species such as blue bush and salt bush, covers the drier parts of the continent. Australian vegetation is generally drought-

[6] Clifford M. Zierer, "The Australian Iron and Steel Industry as a Functional Unit," *Geographical Review*, Vol. 30 (October, 1940), pp. 649–659, and "Industrial Area of Newcastle, Australia," *Economic Geography*, Vol. 17 (1941), pp. 31–49.
[7] Kate L. Mitchell, *An Economic Survey of the Pacific Area*, Part III: *Industrialization of the Western Pacific* (New York, 1942), pp. 241–261.

resistant, nondeciduous, and gray-green in color, thus presenting a somewhat monotonous landscape which differs little in appearance from one time of the year to another.

Australian land forms, too, are lacking in spectacular contrasts. There are no imposing mountain ranges, and broad undulating plains are the most widespread feature. Rivers are comparatively small even in the moist districts, and intermittent streams are characteristic of most parts of the continent. Underground water supplies permit the economic occupation of some places lacking surface streams.

Drought is the most widespread climatic problem in Australia. In much of the interior it is so persistent as to preclude successful human occupation. Elsewhere occasional drought causes widespread losses of livestock and crops. Rainfall in the southern part of the continent falls principally during the winter months, while summers are dry, as in much of California. Along the north coast heavy rains fall during summer months, causing rivers to overflow their banks, while winters are very dry. The eastern coastal district usually receives adequate rainfall throughout the year, which accounts largely for its important population growth and for its agricultural development.

Temperatures are generally high throughout Australia during the summer season, while cool winters characterize the south half. Cold weather and snow are typical only of limited mountain and plateau districts in the southeast.

Rainfall and temperature conditions seriously handicap the spread of population beyond present limits. Many favorable areas now supporting a moderate population are capable of supporting others with more intensive utilization of the land and resources. Most areas not now supporting a moderate population are unlikely to be found capable of supporting appreciable numbers of people in the near future.[8]

---

[8] Griffith Taylor, *Australia: A Study of Warm Environments and Their Effect on British Settlement* (New York, 1940).

The Australian climate invites year-round outdoor activities, and this helps to account for the universal interest in sports. Attractive beaches make the seashore the favorite recreational zone, especially for city folk. Mountain areas likewise provide some relief from higher temperatures, and afford welcome variety in scenery. Tasmania is a popular vacation ground for those on the mainland, especially because of its cooler summers.[9]

Northern Australia is at present of particular interest to Americans because it is from those shores that attacks upon Japanese-held islands may be launched. Darwin, until recently an insignificant port, becomes a possible spearhead for northward attack. Darwin, likewise, assumes new importance in the air age as the gateway to a continent for transoceanic airlines from both Asia and Europe.

Rainfall of 40 to 60 inches occurs at Darwin during the six summer months, November to April, while drought is characteristic of the period from May to October. Temperatures are high throughout the year. Southeast winds with clear skies (favorable for aviation) and somewhat cool nights prevail during the dry season. Hot, sultry weather accompanies the northwest winds during the wet season. Rainfall diminishes rapidly as one travels southward into the interior desert. Stunted and drought-resistant trees and grasses cover the northern coastal region. Cattle raising is the only important local industry, but its output is not large.

Darwin may be reached by a joint railway and highway connection from the south coast near Adelaide. Under normal conditions it is reached only by sea from the principal east-coast centers. The airplane, however, has strikingly improved access to the north coastal district in recent years.

The Northern Territory, of which Darwin is the capital, has long been a "white elephant" so far as economic development is concerned. South Australia poured large sums of money into its development, including the railway to Alice Springs. Despairing of the

[9] Clifford M. Zierer, "Aspects of Urban and Industrial Geography in Tasmania," *Scientific Monthly*, Vol. 53 (October, 1941), pp. 325–345.

task, the Territory was turned over by the state to the Commonwealth in 1909. The railway was never completed beyond Alice Springs, near the center of the continent. Military necessity in 1940, however, led to the building of the 300-mile defense highway to connect Alice Springs with the railway extending southward from Darwin to Birdum. Thus an adequate overland supply route was for the first time made available between the southern cities and the north coast. Distances of 1,500 to 2,000 miles between Darwin and the more productive and populous parts of the continent complicate very seriously the military supply problem.[10]

So long as Australia remains a strong base of Allied power, Japan cannot be secure in southeast Asia. From Australia constant raids upon Japanese outposts and shipping can be made and, as soon as sufficient striking power is accumulated, major offensive operations to the north may be undertaken.

The relationships of New Zealand to the war in the Pacific and her contributions to the Allied Nations' cause are largely based upon geographic conditions. The vast distances which separate her from enemy nations are matched by equal distances which separate her from friendly powers, except Australia, which lies 1,000 miles across the Tasman Sea. New Zealand provides useful bases for naval units of the Allied Nations operating in the southwest Pacific. It is also one of the important links along our supply route to Australia.

New Zealand is a small country with an area of about 100,000 square miles, or the size of Oregon. Its population is 1,600,000 and, as in Australia, it is almost entirely of British extraction. A vigorous aboriginal population is represented by about 90,000 Maoris, of whom at least one-third are mixed with varying proportions of Caucasian blood.[11]

The physical qualities of New Zealand are very different from those of Australia. The Dominion consists chiefly of two compara-

---

[10] C. H. Grattan, *Introducing Australia* (New York, 1942).
[11] Karl J. Pelzer, *An Economic Survey of the Pacific Area*, Part I: *Population and Land Utilization* (New York, 1941), pp. 63–67.

tively rugged islands which lie just within the westerly wind belt. A moist and mild marine climate is characteristic of most lowland areas. The west coast receives more rainfall than the east coast, a fact which makes for contrast in the distribution of native vegetation and of crops and industries.

New Zealand is predominantly a pastoral country with emphasis on dairying and sheep raising. The mild winters and well-distributed rainfall permit the growth of grasses throughout the year and livestock does not require expensive shelters. Butter, frozen meats, and wool comprise the principal export items, most of which have gone to Great Britain in the past. The Canterbury Plain on the drier, eastern side of South Island is an important grain-growing district. The preponderance of comparatively small farm units in New Zealand operated by independent farmers stands out in sharp contrast to the pattern of large land holdings typical of much of Australia.

Forest industries have long been an important factor in New Zealand life. One-fifth of the area remains in forest. An area twice as great has been cleared of forest during the hundred years of European occupation. Extensive areas of high mountain country provide exquisite scenery along the deeply fiorded west coast of South Island. Fishing is an important occupation in the cool waters surrounding New Zealand.

New Zealand's contribution to the war effort is somewhat restricted because of her limited industrial capacity. She lacks a basic iron and steel industry, and in consequence depends upon other nations for most of her arms. New Zealand, however, supplies food, wool, and men for the fighting forces in the southwest Pacific as well as in other theaters of war.

New Zealand is an integral part of the political and economic system which comprises the British Empire. New Zealand's future is bound up closely with that of Australia. In the years ahead, the two nations are likely to coöperate even more closely than in the past, and to the great benefit of both peoples.

Australia and New Zealand are outliers of European civilization in the far corner of the Pacific. They are in no sense Asiatic, nor are they like the South Sea Islands. Indeed, Asiatic and Island influences have been strongly resisted throughout most of the period of white occupation. As C. H. Grattan has said, "Australia is as integral a part of the European-American civilization as if it were situated in the North Atlantic Ocean."[12] The same may be said of New Zealand.

In recent years some Australians and New Zealanders came to recognize that, owing to geographical position, they have special interests and opportunities in the Asiatic sphere. They attempted, for example, to dramatize their proximity to Asia by referring to it as the "Near North." During the 1930's, when European markets were unable to absorb all the products of Australia and New Zealand, large quantities of wool, metals, and other raw materials were exchanged for Japanese manufactures. Some believed that a new era of Australian–Asiatic trade was opening. No other market for Australian raw materials lay nearly so close, and Japan seized the opportunity to enter the Australian markets with her many kinds of manufactured goods. The apparently advantageous trade arrangement, however, proved to be short-lived. The majority of Australians at no time really "relished" their new relationship with Japan.

Only recently, Australia was in imminent danger of being dragged into the orbit of a powerful and aggressive Asiatic nation. Such disaster was probably averted only through prompt assistance rendered by the United States. Australia's relations with Asia in the future doubtless will be moulded in the same economic-political pattern which America and Great Britain formulate. The detailed nature of those relationships can scarcely be forecast at this time. A closer association between Australia and New Zealand, on the one hand, and other Pacific Basin nations is, in all probability, the future trend.

---

[12] "Australia and the Pacific Stalemate," *Asia*, Vol. 41 (March, 1941), pp. 169–171

To the north and northeast of Australia lies an archipelago which connects that continent with Asia. The innumerable islands serve as a series of land bridges between the two continents. Australians have long been deeply concerned over the possibility that the islands might fall into the hands of an unfriendly power. Control of them by friendly nations is considered essential to the defense of the Commonwealth. The Netherlands has long been the principal owner of colonies in that region and has been friendly toward the British Commonwealth of Nations. In fact, she has long depended upon Singapore, Hong Kong, and the British navy for the protection of her own trade routes and her island empire. The interest of the United States in the Philippines has, likewise, for some decades guarded the northern approaches to Australia. The acquisition by Australia of the former German colonies in New Guinea and the Bismarck Archipelago, after the First World War, further strengthened the hand of the British Empire.

In the early 1880's the Australian colonies became seriously concerned about the loosely held islands along her northern frontier. In 1884 the Germans took the initiative and claimed the northeast quarter of New Guinea and the adjacent Bismarck Islands. Great Britain claimed the southeast quarter (Papua) on the basis of Australian defense considerations. In 1905, Papua was transferred to the young Australian Commonwealth. During the years 1914-1918 the German possessions in New Guinea and the Bismarck Islands were occupied by Australian military forces. The areas were assigned as a mandate to Australia in 1920. Australia thus gained control over the whole eastern half of New Guinea while the western half continued to be held by the Netherlands.

New Guinea is the second largest island in the world, being exceeded in size only by Greenland. Its area is in excess of 300,000 square miles. Its greatest length is 1,500 miles and its greatest width more than 400 miles. New Guinea is mountainous in many parts, with ranges along its axis exceeding elevations of 13,000 feet above sea level.

New Guinea has two somewhat indefinite seasons, the wet and the somewhat dry. The wet season is associated with northwest winds which blow during the months November to April. During the period of southeast winds somewhat drier conditions prevail in most localities, although because of topographic conditions some places receive their greatest rainfall during that season. The climate is hot and humid throughout the year and generally unfavorable for Europeans. Dense tropical forests are characteristic of most parts of New Guinea, although extensive savannas occur in some drier lowland districts. Large navigable rivers traverse the island and wide plains are commonly associated with them.

The islands of the Australian Mandate include New Britain, New Ireland, Bougainville (northern Solomons), and numerous smaller groups. The larger islands range in size from 3,000 to 15,000 square miles and all are rugged and forested in most places. Occasional good harbors lend great importance to the islands as naval bases.

New Guinea has a large and vigorous native population engaged principally in primitive subsistence agriculture. Coconut plantations occupy some 300,000 acres in northeastern New Guinea and adjacent islands. Gold has been an important export from the vicinity of Wau, some thirty miles inland from Lae and Salamaua. The few thousand Europeans residing in New Guinea in recent years have been engaged chiefly in plantation management and gold mining. Oil may become a product of commercial importance if encouraging prospects materialize.[13]

Port Moresby, in southeastern New Guinea, has become the principal administrative center for the entire Australian Mandate. Rabaul, at the northern end of New Britain, was the principal center during the period of German control. Commercial development in western New Guinea has been exceedingly small under Dutch control.

---

[13] Stephen Winsor Reed, *The Making of Modern New Guinea* (American Philosophical Society, Memoirs, Vol. 18), 1943.

The Solomon Islands occupy one of the most strategic positions in the southwest Pacific. In Japanese hands they would be a threat to the United States supply lines to Australia. In our hands they can be used as a springboard for attack upon Japanese outposts. If it were not for their strategic position there would be little reason for fighting for the Solomons.

Guadalcanal and other islands in the central Solomons serve as air bases from which attacks can be directed upon Japanese forces in New Britain, New Ireland, and other islands to the north and west. Once the well-defended harbor at Rabaul has been smashed, offensive action against Truk and other military positions in the near-by Japanese Mandate could be undertaken. Such accomplishment would help to remove all threats to the shipping lanes between Hawaii and the southwest Pacific. The Solomons resemble somewhat the islands of the Australian Mandate in topography, climate, vegetation, and native population.

The fall of France raised numerous questions concerning the future of French possessions in the Pacific, some of which are of especial concern to Australia. Our prompt dispatch of armed forces to New Caledonia reflected clearly the importance which we likewise attach to that French possession. Tahiti, and the Marquesas, Tuamotu, and Society groups, are marginal to the main conflict in the Pacific and are of small economic importance. The New Hebrides, controlled jointly by the French and British, are of great strategic importance, serving as a second line of defense behind the Solomons.

New Caledonia lies slightly more than 700 miles from the Australian coast and only about 1,100 miles from New Zealand. In enemy hands it also would serve as a base for attack upon those two countries as well as upon the United States supply lines serving them. Its locational value was illustrated several years ago by the selection of Noumea, capital of New Caledonia, as a port of call by the clipper flying service established by Pan-American Airways between California and Auckland.

New Caledonia is comparatively favorable for white settlement by virtue of its position at the margin of the tropics and because of its somewhat drier climate. Its normal white population of about 15,000 includes many independent farmers in addition to those engaged in mining and in plantation management.

Middle-latitude crops, such as wheat and corn, along with cattle, hogs, sheep, and horses, are important products. Coconuts, coffee, and other tropical products are also raised. About a million acres are utilized for pasturage, and hides and canned meats are regularly exported. Valuable woods are obtained from the island's 1,700,000 acres of forest, including ebony, sandalwood, rosewood, and kauri pine. The area of the island is about 8,500 square miles.

It is the mineral wealth of New Caledonia, however, which accounts chiefly for its international significance. Nickel and chromite are the principal minerals produced and others are likely to be exploited commercially in the future.[14]

Nickel has been the mainstay of the colony's economy for many years. From the opening of the deposits in the 1870's until after 1900, New Caledonia was the world's leading source of supply. Since the discovery of large deposits in Canada that country has normally produced almost nine-tenths of the world's supply. Most of the remainder of the critical alloy metal has continued to come from New Caledonia. Noumea has long been the primary smelting center for ores produced in the island.

The output of chromium, another of the important alloy metals, has risen rapidly in New Caledonia since 1930. Several mines in the northwest part of the island are said to be among the largest in the world. Iron-ore mining was pioneered in New Caledonia by Japan in 1938. The deposit is estimated to contain 20,000,000 tons of ore with 52 per cent iron content.

Three-fourths of the value of normal exports from New Caledonia is in mineral products. Foodstuffs, coal, petroleum products, machinery, and textiles are the usual imports.

---

[14] Jack Shepherd, "New Caledonia—Orphan of the South Pacific," *Pacific Affairs*, Vol. 13 (1940), pp. 423-434.

The alignment of New Caledonia with the Free French in the war against the Axis has continued New Caledonia in close economic association with Australia and the United States. Those countries now absorb the bulk of the mineral output and supply the commodities which must be obtained from the outside.

The New Hebrides form a double chain of islands stretching from northwest to southeast for a distance of more than 500 miles. They have an area of 5,700 square miles, of which 1,500 are in Santo, the principal island. The larger islands are of volcanic origin and mountainous (maximum elevation over 6,000 feet). The coastlines are very irregular and at least four good harbors are available in the group. The climate of the New Hebrides, like that in other parts of Melanesia, is hot, moist, and enervating. Malaria is a common disease and amoebic dysentery is widespread.

Some 60,000 native Melanesians reside in the New Hebrides, along with about 2,000 French and British plantation operators and missionaries. Since 1906, control of the islands has been under joint French and British control. The administrative center is at Vila on the island of Efate. Vila is situated on a fine harbor and is the chief commercial center of the group. The products of the New Hebrides are chiefly agricultural, and include copra, cacao, cotton, coffee, maize, and tropical fruits. Most of the trade is conducted through Sydney, Australia, although some is carried on directly with European countries.[15]

The colony of Fiji, to the east of the New Hebrides, consists of about 250 islands with a total area of 7,083 square miles. The islands range in size from Viti Levu with an area of 4,053 square miles to tiny, rocky islands without habitation. About 80 islands are permanently inhabited. The total population is slightly more than 200,000 persons, of whom half are native Fijians and the remainder Indians, except for a few thousand Europeans and other immigrants. Suva, the capital and chief commercial center, has a population of about 15,000. It is second in shipping only to Honolulu among the

[15] R. W. Robson, ed., *The Pacific Islands Year Book*, 1939 (Sydney), pp. 139–151.

Pacific island ports and is commonly referred to as the "crossroads of the South Pacific."

The larger islands are commonly hilly or mountainous, rising abruptly to heights of 3,000 or 4,000 feet from the sea. Rainfall is abundant, vegetation is dense, and some rivers are of large size. Much fertile soil is found along the larger rivers where wide valleys have been carved through volcanic materials.

Most islands are surrounded by a barrier reef of coral, but passages usually occur opposite river mouths. Between the reef and the shore ships may lie safely at anchor protected by the natural breakwater. The forests contain many valuable species of commercial timber. Gold has been an important mineral product of the islands in recent years.

The climate is controlled by the southeast trades, which blow more or less steadily throughout the year. The windward sides of the larger islands are extremely wet, while on the lee sides much less rainfall is received and a marked dry season proves helpful to the planter. Hurricane winds with heavy rainfall frequently prove very destructive to crops and buildings.

Fiji is one of the economically more important island groups in the southwest Pacific. The long-established sugar industry is the backbone of the island economy and copra production is also highly significant. Bananas are the principal tropical fruit grown and important shipments go to New Zealand and also to Canada. Cattle production is steadily growing in importance. Foodstuffs of wide variety are produced in sufficient quantities to meet island requirements. Manufactured goods such as textiles, machinery, motor vehicles, and fuels are the principal imports.

The large Indian population is engaged principally in the sugar industry, having been imported originally as coolie laborers. Native Fijians, although of fine physique and experienced as agriculturists, could not be induced to become plantation laborers. Many Indians also live in Suva, where they are small shopkeepers and artisans. Little diffusion takes place between Indians and Fijians because each regards the other as inferior. Three-fourths of the Indians were born in Fiji. "The little India of the South Pacific" is a descriptive title sometimes applied to Fiji.[16]

The islands of Melanesia, that is, New Guinea, New Britain, the Solomons, New Caledonia, the New Hebrides, and Fiji, form a major protective arc off the northeast coast of Australia. Most of them are comparatively large islands, and are in the main mountainous and densely wooded. They are sufficiently large to afford bases for military operations of some magnitude. Numerous good harbors are available for naval forces among the islands. Airfields can be widely distributed, thus affording the advantage of dispersal of the air arm. Dense vegetation makes enemy observation of military activities somewhat difficult. Water supply is no special problem and local foodstuffs may be drawn upon for the military forces. Natives constitute an important labor force. Port Moresby, Rabaul, Noumea, and Suva are capable of serving as the naval outposts of the southwest Pacific after the pattern of Honolulu and Dutch Harbor in the northeast Pacific.

The Netherlands Indies is the most productive and valuable tropical region in all the world. Its thousands of islands have a total land area of 734,000 square miles, or one-fourth that of the continental United States and more than fifty times that of Holland. The archipelago stretches for 3,200 miles in a broad belt along the equator. The Indies control the strategic passageways between the Pacific and Indian oceans and the most important trade route between East Asia and Europe.

The climate of the Indies is tropical, with high temperatures and abundant rainfall prevailing throughout the year. High volcanic mountain ranges with dense forests form the backbones of many of the islands. Rich soils derived from basic volcanic materials help to account for the exceptional productivity of certain lowland districts. Poorer soils and rugged relief account for the scant development of many of the outlying islands.

---

[16] John W. Coulter, *Fiji: Little India of the Pacific* (Chicago, 1942).

The aggregate population of the Indies is more than 70,000,000, or approximately equal to that of Japan. Two-thirds of the population is concentrated in Java and Madura alone, one-sixth in Sumatra, and the remaining one-sixth is widely scattered among the other islands. While Java and Madura have only 7 per cent of land area of the Indies, they have about 70 per cent of the people. The average density of population in Java and Madura is about 800 persons per square mile, which is the more remarkable because it is based upon agricultural development alone. Densities of about 25 persons per square mile are characteristic of the Outer Islands. The large percentage of cultivated land in Java and Madura, the widespread and intensive production of rice, and the employment of many persons on commercial plantations help to explain the ability of those islands to support such great numbers of people.

Europeans comprise less than one-half of one per cent (240,000) of the population of the Indies, but they exert an economic and political influence which far exceeds their numerical ratio. They are concentrated principally in Java and Madura. Chinese are five times as numerous as Europeans (1,233,000) and are widely scattered throughout the Indies, principally as tradespeople.

Population has grown phenomenally in the Indies (about tenfold) during the period of Dutch administration. Cessation of tribal warfare, the application of modern medicine, and the development of commercial agriculture have been important contributory factors to population increase. The inequitable distribution of population between Java and Madura, on the one hand, and the Outer Islands, on the other, comprises one of the major problems in the colony.[17]

The Netherlands Indies is the world's most important producer of tropical agricultural products. The islands have enjoyed a virtual monopoly in the production of cinchona bark, from which quinine is made, accounting for 90 per cent of the world output

---

[17] Karl J. Pelzer, *An Economic Survey of the Pacific Area*, Part I: *Population and Land Utilization* (New York, 1941); Jack Shepherd, "Netherlands India's Neglected Islands," *Far Eastern Survey*, Vol. 9 (July 17, 1940), pp. 71–77.

in 1939. In 1938 the Indies supplied 85 per cent of the world's pepper exports, 63 per cent of the kapok, 33 per cent of the rubber, 29 per cent of the copra, 27 per cent of the cordage, 24 per cent of the palm oil, and 17 per cent of the world's tea exports. In addition, it exported substantial amounts of sugar, spices, coffee, tapioca, tobacco, and other tropical products. Minerals are important, too, among the products of the Indies, especially tin and petroleum. The islands are in some ways closely associated economically with Malaya, Indo-China, Thailand, and Burma on the Asiatic mainland. Together, these regions have produced practically all the world's output of natural rubber and three-fourths of the tin. They also produce most of the world's export rice.

American trade with the Indies was increasing steadily prior to the Japanese occupation. In 1939 the United States supplied the Indies with 13 per cent of its imports and stood third among the countries sending goods there. In the same year the United States took 20 per cent of the exports from the Indies and also stood third among countries buying goods from the islands.[18] The Netherlands Indies has been of increasing importance for the investment of American capital, although our investments are small in comparison with those of the Dutch and British. Since the United States has long been the principal user of rubber and tin, free commercial access to those areas is a matter of prime importance.

The Philippines lie only forty-three miles across narrow straits to the north of the Netherlands Indies. More than seven thousand mountainous and tropical islands, thirty of which have areas of 100 square miles or more, support a population of 16,000,000 persons. Luzon and Mindanao are the principal islands, and the former supports most of the population. Mindanao and some of the smaller islands are capable of supporting many additional people. As in the Indies, maldistribution of population rather than overpopulation comprises one of the principal problems.

[18] Katherine R. C. Greene and Joseph D. Phillips, *An Economic Survey of the Pacific Area*, Part II: *Transportation and Foreign Trade* (New York, 1942), pp. 165–167.

More than 55 per cent of the area of the Philippines remains under forest cover. Little more than one-fifth of the total area is included in farms and estates, of which probably only 65 per cent is actually cultivated. Nearly three-fifths of the crop acreage is devoted to rice and corn. Other important crops are coconuts, sugar cane, abaca, tobacco, and maguey. Double cropping is widely practiced but is capable of further extension. Irrigation is much less utilized than in crowded mainland countries. Shifting native agriculture is typical of hilly regions and creates extensive areas of coarse grassland which previously supported dense tropical forests. Shifting cultivation is also a cause of serious local soil wastage.

The encouragement of estate or plantation agriculture under European and American stimulus has greatly increased the output of agricultural export commodities, but it has also contributed to a serious tenantry problem. A considerable amount of the Philippines' contributions to world markets in recent decades must be attributed to the political relationship to the United States.

Trade and investments are important factors in American interest in the Netherlands Indies and in the Philippines. Americans do not propose to allow a power bent on continental and world conquest to gain exclusive control over vast supplies of strategic raw materials and important markets for manufactured goods. Furthermore, the fate of China and the small mainland countries of southeast Asia is involved along with that of the island groups. The Allied Nations are pledged to the restoration of their free contact with all the world.

Since the voyages of Captain James Cook, the people of the English-speaking world have been intrigued by stories of the South Sea Islands. Since the outbreak of war in the Pacific those specks of land have taken on exceptional importance, strategically. Resembling the manner in which they served as stopping points for early mariners plotting their courses across the Pacific, those islands now serve as steppingstones for transoceanic flights. While the sailing ship, and especially the modern liner, were attracted chiefly to those islands which possess good harbors, the airman needs only a sufficient amount of level ground for a landing strip and accessory facilities. Thus tiny uninhabited specks of land barely above the ocean surface, if situated along prospective air routes, suddenly take on international significance. Islets long considered too small to claim become important stations in a worldwide system of aerial transport.

The South Sea Islands, as here defined, stretch over a vast triangular oceanic area from Hawaii and the French possessions, in the northeast and southeast respectively, to the Japanese Mandate on the west. They include most of Polynesia and Micronesia as outlined by the anthropologist. All of them are tropical, but those farthest from the equator are made more livable by the trade winds which blow during at least part of the year. The vast expanse of sea over which these islands are distributed exerts its influence upon them in many ways. Most important of all, perhaps, the ocean provides an isolation which lends a unique character to the islands themselves and to their inhabitants.

Most of the islands are coralline, very restricted in extent, low in elevation, and capable of supporting only limited vegetation and population. Some of the islands with volcanic cores rise to greater heights and afford somewhat larger variety in land forms and rainfall conditions.

Because of their isolated positions, their limited extent and restricted resources, life on them is actually far from ideal. A garden type of agriculture has long been the primary basis of livelihood for the natives. Coconut palms, which fringe the shorelines of most islands, provide the staff of life. Since there is little space or feed for domestic animals, only pigs and fowls are common. The sea and the enclosed lagoon are important sources of supplementary food. Soils derived from coral are relatively shallow and usually infertile. Water supplies are restricted and, if derived from wells, usually saline. Hurricanes add to the hazards of existence in some places.

The South Seas region is of some importance in supplying raw materials to middle-latitude nations. Tropical plantations have been established by outside peoples, although some of those adventures have not been very successful. Copra, phosphate, sugar, and tropical fruits are the principal exports of the islands. Manufactured goods from middle-latitude countries find limited markets among the island peoples. The exchange of glass beads for the wealth of the islands, however, is a form of trade existing chiefly in the minds of imaginative writers. Trade goods which natives seek and for which they bargain rather shrewdly are metal tools, matches, household utensils, cloth, and the like.

While native populations are dominant in most of the island groups, scattered minorities of European and (or) Asiatic extraction are present nearly everywhere. Hybrid races are an increasingly significant element. Overpopulation is a problem in some of the smaller islands. The attractions of the port centers have drawn many of the younger set from native agricultural pursuits and made them victims of an uncertain money economy.

The future of the peoples of the South Seas is bound up with the destinies of powerful claimant nations in distant parts of the world. European powers, in the days of imperialism, overlooked few of the island groups. More recently, the nations bordering the Pacific Basin have stressed their claims upon islands deemed essential to mainland security. Eight different nations lay claim to various parts of the island world.[19]

Australia has participated to an increasing degree in the commercial life of certain of the island groups. Japan has vigorously developed her Mandate islands within the decade, and has penetrated much farther to the south with capital investments and shipping facilities. American interests have gone far in converting Hawaii into an outpost of middle-latitude industrialization.

The colonial claims of the European powers are certain to be vigorously pressed in the air age. The claims of nations bordering

[19] F. M. Keesing, *The South Seas in the Modern World* (New York, 1941).

the Pacific for islands which they regard as indispensable for their security are certain to be an important consideration in whatever political arrangements come out of the present world conflict.

The Pacific Basin is a region of dynamic political, economic, and social activity. Every segment of it is undergoing significant change. The Pacific Basin is a great new frontier for the present generation of Americans. It does not offer to young Americans vast new lands for settlement, for most parts of it are already fully occupied. It affords, instead, new frontiers for trade with independent peoples. It provides an opportunity for the development of an international scheme under which nations of diverse cultures may live peacefully together. No nation has a greater opportunity for helping to shape the future of the Pacific Basin than the United States of America.

# PEOPLES AND CULTURES OF THE SOUTHWEST PACIFIC

---

### HARRY HOIJER
ASSISTANT PROFESSOR OF ANTHROPOLOGY
IN THE UNIVERSITY OF CALIFORNIA

*Lecture delivered April 5, 1943*

# PEOPLES AND CULTURES OF THE SOUTHWEST PACIFIC

IN FEW discussions of the war in the South Pacific do we find mention of the aboriginal peoples of that area. One might think that the region was barren of all save Europeans, Americans, and Asiatics of the more advanced civilizations. Yet the islands of the South Pacific, with few exceptions, have large and important native populations, distinctive in physical type and possessing languages and cultures widely divergent from those of Europe, America, and Asia. We cannot hope to extend successfully the principles and ideals of our modern world civilization to Oceania without taking these peoples into account. Any policy which seeks to do so is doomed to failure; witness the general bankruptcy of colonial administrations in the South Pacific and the neighboring Asiatic mainland today.

The following sketch seeks to summarize, very briefly, some of the essential facts about the peoples and cultures of Oceania. It makes no claim to originality; the writer has had, of necessity, to depend upon the work of those who have had living experience in the area. Nor is it claimed that the summary is exhaustive; information on Oceania is still being accumulated. But there is in the following pages enough to illustrate the variety and wealth of cultural behavior to be found in the South Pacific and to emphasize the complexity of the problems confronting those who would work in the area.

Finally, it may be pointed out that the cultures described are those which prevailed in Oceania before extensive contact with the whites had taken place. In some regions, such as the Solomon Islands and the interior of New Guinea, such contacts have not yet seriously modified the native cultures; in others, for example Hawaii, the Philippines, and Australia, much of the overt aboriginal culture has been profoundly modified by European and American contacts. But in either case the native aboriginal civilizations are not to be ignored, for it is on these bases that many of the present-day cultures of the South Pacific rest. And we must understand the background of native civilization before an adequate study of the problems of the present period can successfully be undertaken.

*The Land.*—The region of the Southwest Pacific, called Oceania by anthropologists, comprises all the territory situated between the southeastern coast of Asia and the coastline of the Americas. In terms of the aboriginal inhabitants and their cultures this region is customarily divided into five principal subareas: (1) Australia and Tasmania, (2) Malaysia or Indonesia, (3) Melanesia, (4) Micronesia, and (5) Polynesia.

Most of the interior of Australia has a semiarid desert climate which gives way to grasslands and savannas as one moves to the north and east. Along the eastern and southeastern coasts are found temperate forests, and these too are found over most of the island of Tasmania, lying off the southeastern coast of Australia and separated from it by Bass Strait. The fauna and flora of both Australia and Tasmania indicate that the region has long been isolated from the continent of Asia and from the neighboring islands. Indeed, it seems quite certain that this subarea of Oceania was isolated from the rest of the world as early as the mid-Pleistocene and that it remained so until the discovery by Europeans in the early eighteenth century.

Malaysia is composed of the island groups north of Australia lying between the Asiatic coast and New Guinea. Some of the principal island groups are: the Sunda Islands (Sumatra, Java, Bali, and others), Borneo, Celebes, the Spice Islands, the Philippines, and Formosa. In addition, most anthropologists would include the Malay Peninsula and the Andaman and Nicobar Islands of the Bay of Bengal in the territory of Malaysia. Finally, it should be mentioned that the Malagasy of Madagascar, though geographically remote from Malaysia, are very similar to the Malay in race, language, and culture, and undoubtedly derive from the same source historically.

Most of the Malaysian area is covered by heavy tropical rain forest not very different from that found on the neighboring mainland. Similarly, the fauna of Malaysia, as well as its aboriginal inhabitants and their cultures, indicate a contact of long standing with the mainland of Asia. This contact, as will be made clear later, has considerably affected both the physical type and the ways of life of the Malaysians, particularly in the islands of Sumatra, Java, and Bali.

Melanesia is sometimes divided into two areas: (1) Papua or New Guinea, and (2) the islands extending to the southeast, the Bismarck Archipelago, the Solomon Islands, the Santa Cruz Islands, the New Hebrides, and the Loyalties. The Fiji Islands, east and a bit north of the Loyalties, are Melanesian in physical type but dominantly Polynesian in culture.

Like Malaysia, most of the Melanesian islands are continental in vegetation and climate. In New Guinea, however, there are a number of animals which suggest an early connection with Australia—a suggestion which is partly borne out by similarities in culture as well. In the rest of Melanesia neither the fauna nor the cultures tie in with those of Australia or Malaysia.

East of the Philippines, between the equator and the Tropic of Cancer, are the numerous coral islands comprising Micronesia. The principal groups are: the Marianas, the Caroline Islands, the Marshalls, and the Gilberts. The two last-named groups form the eastern boundary of Micronesia. In this region we find an entirely different climate, vegetation, and fauna. The climate is Oceanic rather than continental, and both vegetation and fauna are extremely sparse. Indeed, except for a few plants and animals of little or no significance economically, most of the fauna and flora found there today are believed to have been carried to Micronesia by the aboriginal inhabitants.

Much of Polynesia is similar to Micronesia in respect to climate, fauna, and flora. On some of the larger islands, however, we find a climate and vegetation not dissimilar to that of Melanesia. Polynesia extends in a broad arc from Hawaii to Easter Island (less than 2,000 miles from the coast of South America) to New Zealand. Some of the more important island groups included are: the Marquesas, the Phoenix Islands, the Ellice Islands, Samoa, Tonga, the Society Islands, and Tuamotu or the Low Archipelago.

*The People.*—The peoples of the world fall into four major groups racially, the criteria by which they are distinguished being solely anatomical. These grand divisions of mankind are: (1) the Caucasoids, including most of the races of present-day Europe and America; (2) the Negroids, found principally in Africa but also, in smaller enclaves, in America and Oceania; (3) the Mongoloids, centering in eastern Asia but found as well in eastern Europe, Oceania, and in aboriginal America; and (4) the Composite Races, groups which represent more or less stabilized mixtures of two or three of the main lines described in the preceding divisions. Though scattered groups of such mixed populations occur wherever contact between races belonging to two distinct grand divisions has been long continued, the bulk of the Composite Races are to be found in Oceania.

The Oceanic peoples belong to two of the four grand divisions of mankind, the Negroid and the Composite. There are four Negroid races in Oceania: (1) the Negritos or Dwarfed Blacks, who live in the Andaman Islands, the interior of the Malay Peninsula, one or two islands of the Philippines, and the remote interior of New Guinea; (2) the Tasmanians, now extinct, who formerly occupied the entire island of Tasmania; (3) the Papuans in the interior regions of New Guinea; and (4) the Melanesians, who occupy the coasts of New Guinea and the other islands of Melanesia. The two last-named races are very similar and probably represent a recent divergence from an earlier common stock. The Papuans, who are more Negroid in type, are presumably closer to the ancestral stock; the Melanesians possess a number of traits indicative of Mongoloid admixture.

All these Negroid races possess traits which link them to the

Negroid races of Africa and America, but each possesses, as well, certain distinctive traits which appear in no other Negroid race and serve to distinguish them as separate races. Thus, for example, the Negrito is roundheaded or brachycephalic in contrast to the longheadedness of all other Negroids and is very much shorter in stature, averaging 4 ft. 9 in. or less. In the accompanying table (table 1)[1] each of the Oceanic Negroid races is compared with the Forest Negro of Africa in those traits in which the five races differ most markedly. It may be noted here, too, that Negritos, essentially similar anatomically to those of Oceania, are also found in the Congo forest of Africa. The other Oceanic Negroids appear to be confined to these regions.

Four composite races are found in Oceania: the aboriginal Australians, the Indonesians, the Malays, and the Polynesians. The Australians are confined to the continent of Australia and are probably derived from an ancient Caucasoid people who mixed, in very early times, with a Negroid people, possibly the precursors of the Tasmanians. Both archaeological and somatological evidences support this conclusion. Extreme longheadedness, small cranial capacity, low, retreating foreheads, and enormous brow ridges are traits of the modern Australian which link him to much earlier and more archaic forms of men, while skeletal forms unearthed in Australia and in Java suggest a link between the modern Australian and ancient Pleistocene forms.[2] In this connection, it is of interest to note that the flora and fauna of Australia, as well as its human inhabitants, suggest that Australia was cut off from all connection with the Asiatic mainland as early as the mid-Pleistocene and remained isolated until the beginning of the eighteenth century.

The Caucasoid strain in the modern Australian is evidenced especially by his abundant face, head, and body hair and by the fact that his hair is wavy or curly (see table 2). The Negroid admixture exhibits itself in his dark skin, hair, and eyes, his broad and short

---

[1] The data presented in tables 1 and 2 has been taken, in large part, from E. A. Hooton, *Up From the Ape* (New York, 1931), pp. 512–515, 516–520.
[2] E. A. Hooton, *op. cit.*, pp. 552–553.

TABLE 1

CHARACTERISTICS OF NEGROID RACES

| Trait | Forest Negro of Africa | Negrito | Tasmanian | Melanesian | Papuan |
|---|---|---|---|---|---|
| Head | Dolichocephalic; narrow head, marked occipital protrusion. Little or no brow ridge. | Brachycephalic; forehead bulging. No brow ridges. | Dolichocephalic. | Dolichocephalic; large continuous brow ridges; marked occipital protrusion. | |
| Nose and lips | Nose broad and short, Lips thick, everted, full, and red. | Nose very broad and short. Lips of medium thickness, not greatly everted, upper lip long. | Nose very broad and short. Lips of medium thickness. | Nose prominent and hooked; long and broad. Lips less thick and everted than those of the Forest Negro. | Nose longer and more hooked than that of the Melanesian. |
| Other facial features | Face long and somewhat broad; marked facial protrusion. | Same as for Forest Negro. | Face very short and rather broad; medium facial protrusion. | Face long and somewhat broad; marked facial protrusion. | |
| Pigmentation | Hair black; eyes and skin dark brown to black. | Hair black; eyes and skin dark brown to black. | Hair and eyes black; skin dark brown to black. | Hair black; eyes dark brown to black. Skin dark brown to black, the Melanesian being as a rule lighter in skin color than the Papuan. | |
| Hair | Woolly or frizzly; coarse, wiry, and short; beard and body hair sparse. | Woolly or frizzly; often peppercorn; coarse, wiry, and short; beard and body hair sparse. | Woolly or frizzly; coarse, wiry, and short; beard and body hair sparse. | More often frizzly; occasionally long and frizzly hair; beard and body hair sparse. | More often woolly; shorter than Melanesian; beard and body hair sparse. |
| Stature and body build | Medium to tall (5 ft. 7 in. or more). Broad, heavy torso; long arms, relatively short legs. | Very short (4 ft. 9 in. or less). Infantile body, narrow shoulders, short legs, pot bellies. | Medium stature (5 ft. 5 in.). | Tall and well proportioned. | Shorter than Melanesian; well-proportioned. |

nose, and his thick lips. The source of this Negroid strain is unknown, but it is suggested that it came as a result of contact with the precursors of the Tasmanians who presumably reached their island by way of Australia.[3]

In the Malay Peninsula and Indonesia are found two other composite races, the Indonesian and the Malay. The Indonesian race, which appears to be dominantly Caucasoid (of the Mediterranean or "dark" Caucasoid variety) plus an admixture of southern Mongoloid and Negroid blood, is found mostly in the inland areas of Malaysia. Malays are very similar to Indonesians, but are dominantly of southern Mongoloid extraction with Mediterranean Caucasoid and Negroid admixture. These people are most numerous in Malaysia and live for the most part in the coastal areas.

Historically, it has been suggested that a Negroid race, possibly the precursors of the Negritos, were the first modern race to inhabit Malaysia. These peoples were in large part driven out by invaders from southeastern Asia, dominantly Mediterranean in blood but with some Mongoloid admixture. Since the invaders undoubtedly acquired some Negroid blood from the people they drove away, this would give us the modern Indonesians. Lastly, the Indonesians were reduced in numbers and driven to the inland areas by a wave of southern Mongoloid invaders who mixed with the Indonesian to form the modern Malay. Some of the Negroid admixture in both the Indonesian and the Malay may of course be due to the Oceanic Negroids of Melanesia who, in all probability, passed through the southern islands of Indonesia in their passage to the regions they now occupy.

The more important physical characteristics of the Indonesian and Malay are contrasted in table 2. It is especially to be noted that the Malay contrasts with the Indonesian in head form, the shape of the face, hair texture, and body build. In all these traits the Malay is distinctively closer to the Mongoloid than is the Indonesian.

The rest of Oceania is occupied by the fourth of our composite

---
[3] *Ibid.*

## TABLE 2
### Characteristics of Australian, Indonesian, Malay, and Polynesian Peoples

| Trait | Australian | Indonesian | Malay | Polynesian |
|---|---|---|---|---|
| Head | Extremely dolichocephalic; small cranial capacity; low, retreating forehead; brow ridges largest for all extant races and continuous across forehead. | Dolicho- or mesocephalic; no brow ridges. | Brachycephalic; no brow ridges. | Generally brachycephalic but sometimes meso- or dolichocephalic. Slight or no brow ridges. |
| Nose and lips | Nose very broad and short—platyrrhine. Lips of medium thickness. | Flat concave nose—meso- or platyrrhine. Lips of medium thickness. | Flatter and more Mongoloid than those of the Indonesian—meso- or platyrrhine. Lips of medium thickness. | High, broad nose, concave or straight. Usually mesobut sometimes lepto- or platyrrhine. Lips of medium thickness. |
| Other facial features | Face of medium width but very short; accentuated facial prognathism. | Face longer and less square than that of the Malay; cheek bones less projecting. Mongoloid "slanted" eyes less frequent. Little or no prognathism. | Broad, short faces, projecting cheekbones; flat faces. Some occurrence of Mongoloid "slanting" eyes. Little or no prognathism. | Long and broad faces; prominent cheek bones with fatty covering. Occasional long, narrow faces. Very slight facial prognathism. |
| Pigmentation | Hair black to dark brown; eyes and skin dark brown. | Hair usually black, but sometimes has reddish tinge; eyes dark brown; skin brown to yellow-brown. | Same as that of the Indonesian. | Dark brown hair and eyes Skin yellow-brown. |
| Hair | Wavy to curly hair; abundant face, head, and body hair. The hairiest of all races. | Hair usually has a slight wave; hair abundant on head, sparse on face and body. | Straight, coarse hair; abundant on head, sparse on face and body. | Hair usually wavy, sometimes straight; abundant on head, scant on face and body. |
| Stature and body build | Medium stature (5 ft. 6 in.). Slender body, short trunk, long legs. | Short in stature (5 ft. 1 in.). Slender body, less squat and square than that of the Malay. | Short in stature (5 ft. 1 in.). Squat and thickset body. | Tall in stature (5 ft. 7 in.). Well-proportioned body. |

races, the Polynesian. These peoples live on the islands of Micronesia and Polynesia. The bulk of the Polynesians are a trihybrid race in which some Mediterranean Caucasoid racial strain is outstanding, a southern Mongoloid admixture is clear, and there is a perceptible strain of either Melanesian or Negrito blood.[4] Because of this trihybrid character there is a good deal of variability in the anatomical characteristics of the Polynesian. The distinctive traits are listed in table 2 and give a basis for comparison with the other composite racial groups of Oceania.

There are two main lines of travel whereby the Polynesians may have reached the areas in which they now live. They may have come from southeastern Asia through the southernmost islands of Indonesia and the Melanesian chain, or they may have come from Asia through Micronesia and so out to the Polynesian islands. It is probable that both routes were employed but that the greater part of the Polynesians used the Micronesian line of migration. This would account for the fact that the Negroid strain is least perceptible in the Micronesian Polynesians and in those of northern Polynesia, and more marked in the Polynesians living in New Zealand and the islands to the east of Fiji.

*The Languages.*—Most of the languages spoken in Oceania belong to the widespread Malayo-Polynesian family. The exceptions to this rule are as follows: the languages of Australia, which appear to be interrelated though no relationship to languages elsewhere has yet been established; the Tasmanian languages, now extinct, which may have been remotely related to those of Australia; the languages of the Andaman Islands, interrelated but so far isolated from all others; the so-called Papuan languages of the interior of New Guinea, which are not only unrelated to any other group but have not yet been shown to be interrelated; and a few scattered languages of the Nicobar Islands and the Malay Peninsula which appear to belong to the Mon Khmer stock centered in Indo-China.

The Malayo-Polynesian family has several subdivisions: Ma-

---
[4] *Ibid.*, p. 520.

layan, spoken in Malaysia and Madagascar; Melanesian, spoken throughout Melanesia except in the area occupied by the Papuans; Micronesian; and Polynesian. In spite of the vast area covered by the speakers of these languages, they are very similar to one another and the interrelationship is undisputed. In recent times, Malay (of the Malayan group) has become a *lingua franca* for most of Oceania and is therefore the most important idiom. Pidgin English, a curious minimal language with a vocabulary largely English but a highly simplified grammatical structure, is also used as a *lingua franca*.

The great expanse covered by the Malayo-Polynesian languages and their relatively slight differentiation suggests that the speakers of these languages have spread over Oceania in comparatively recent times. Contrariwise, we may note that the Australian, Andaman, and Papuan languages are restricted in distribution and are very diverse, thus permitting the inference that the speakers of these languages are older in Oceania than the speakers of Malayo-Polynesian. Note, too, that the Melanesian Negroids speak Malayo-Polynesian languages while the Papuans do not. It is quite possible, therefore, that the Melanesians acquired their languages, as well as their Mongoloid blood, from later Malayo-Polynesian-speaking invaders, and that earlier in their history they spoke languages more nearly related to those of the Papuans. A similar loss of their earlier speech may be suggested for the Negritos, who everywhere, except in the Andamans where they have long been isolated, speak the language of their nearest neighbors.

*The Material Culture.*—By material culture is meant the technology or the economy of a people, the totality of the techniques whereby they achieve an adjustment to the environment in which they live.[5] A technology may best be described in terms of three techniques which appear to be basic and upon which all other techniques apparently depend: the types of cutting tool used, the methods of obtaining food, and the means of transportation.[6]

---

[5] E. C. Chapple and C. S. Coon, *Principles of Anthropology* (New York, 1942), p. 223.
[6] *Ibid.*, p. 224.

Viewing Oceania as a whole with respect to the development of these basic techniques, it is possible to divide the area, very roughly, into five major divisions: (1) Australia, Tasmania, the Andaman Islands, and certain scattered and isolated peoples of Malaysia; (2) the Papuans of New Guinea; (3) the Melanesians; (4) the Polynesians and Micronesians; and (5) the Malaysians.

1) Australia, Tasmania, and the Andamans.—Most, if not all, of the societies in this area are isolated from the main streams of cultural innovation by geographical or other barriers.[7] Tools and weapons are made of sharp-edged shells, the teeth of animals, fire-hardened wood, or crudely chipped flints. The Tasmanians employ the simplest techniques; here, flint is fractured by smashing a lump of it on another rock and selecting from the fragments those which have sharp edges or points. Some stone polishing or grinding is done by the Australians, and more advanced techniques of chipping flint are found here as well. Among the Andamanese it has been noted that scrap iron, obtained from wrecked ships which drift near the shore, is also used to make cutting tools. For all, however, it may be stated that toolmaking as an art is definitely retarded—that little advance over the Europeans of the Paleolithic may be noted.

As a result, other aspects of the material culture are similarly retarded. Weapons are mainly the spear and the club; the bow and arrow occur only among the Andamans. Shelters vary from simple windbreaks of piled brush to crude structures of interwoven branches covered with leaves. Clothing is often lacking and, where present, is made of leaves, bark cloth, or poorly cured skins. Containers are few: wooden troughs, bags of netting, simple baskets, and natural containers of shell and sections of bamboo stalk.

Domestication, either of plants or animals, is unknown among these peoples. All food is gathered from the wilds: roots, nuts, insects, small animals, shellfish, and the like. Hunting is often im-

---

[7] The so-called "ethnological present" is used for the sake of convenience. As has already been pointed out, some of the cultures to be described are partly or wholly extinct whereas others are still functioning though in more or less modified form.

portant, larger animals such as the kangaroo, the wallaby, and, in the Andamans, the pig and the turtle, being secured in this fashion. Fishing is done over most of the area; it is lacking only in Tasmania. Both hunting and fishing, however, are usually performed by individuals alone; coöperative effort in these occupations is rare or lacking.

Because of these food-acquiring techniques, and because much of the territory in which these peoples live is none too well supplied with wild foods, these societies are obliged to lead a nomadic existence, moving from place to place within a certain district. There are, then, no settled villages, but only temporary or semipermanent camps. Density of population is low for the same reasons.

Land transport is entirely by human carrier; even where the dog is tamed, as in Australia, he is not used as a beast of burden. Usually, watercraft are lacking, though among some peoples, as for example the Tasmanians, very crudely constructed boats are found, useful only for coastal travel well within sight of land.

2) The Papuans of New Guinea.—The Papuans of New Guinea have a material culture quite a good deal richer than that which has just been described. Here we find that polished stone tools are dominant, stone chipping being rare or lacking. Another important addition is bamboo; slit lengthwise, pieces of bamboo serve very adequately for knives and other edged tools. Metals, however, are lacking.

The bow and arrow, spear, club, and daggers made of bone are the principal weapons. Shelters are variable: some are one-family dwellings set on piles or in trees; others are large communal houses. All, however, are permanent or semipermanent dwellings well constructed of hardwood logs and bamboo. The houses are grouped in villages, often stockaded. One or more houses may be for ceremonial purposes exclusively; these are often large and elaborately decorated. Clothing is scanty: gourd or shell penis covers for the men, and fiber aprons for the women. The hair, particularly of the men, may be elaborately dressed and both sexes are likely to wear numerous ornaments and to decorate their bodies in complex designs formed by scarifying the flesh. Containers are made of pottery, wood, netting, and basketry.

Among the Papuans agriculture is the primary means of subsistence. Hunting is of some importance in certain regions and, along the coasts, fishing may also play a part in the food quest. Chickens and pigs are domesticated and used for food. Cannibalism, primarily of a ritual nature, is widespread.

The basic crops are yams, taro, breadfruit, and bananas. Sago, the pith of a certain palm tree, is collected and prepared for food. Garden plots are usually prepared by cutting away the underbrush and trees, burning the wood, and using the ash as fertilizer. In the highland regions of the interior, fields may be terraced and irrigation practiced where necessary. In addition to the foods already mentioned, betel nut (from the areca palm) is collected and chewed with pepper leaves and lime as a narcotic. Tobacco is also grown, though this is a relatively recent borrowing from Europeans; it is smoked in pipes and cigarettes.

There is some specialization by villages in crops raised and in handicrafts. Trade between neighboring villages is therefore important, one village exchanging its specialty for that of another. Along the coasts, travel is by canoe, but these are crudely made and suited only for coastal travel. In the interior, foot trails are maintained between villages, with suspension bridges over the rivers and bridges of arched bamboo over the smaller streams.

3) *The Melanesians.*—The material cultures of Melanesia are quite similar to the Papuan cultures just described, particularly with respect to cutting tools, containers, and shelters. Clothing is also not markedly different, though bark cloth is probably more widely used as a material.

With respect to methods of securing food, however, there is an important difference between Melanesians and Papuans. Like the Papuans, the Melanesians raise yams, taro, breadfruit, and bananas, collect sago and betel nut, and have domesticated the chicken and the pig for food; but, being wholly a coastal and island people, they are expert canoemen and depend as much on fish and other products of the sea as they do on their crops and domestic animals. Specialization, particularly in handicrafts, is also more marked among the Melanesians, with a resulting more intensive development of trade. Since the Melanesians rarely travel overland, most of this trade is carried on between islands and by water. Their boats are large, well made, and quite seaworthy. There are three principal types: the outrigger canoe, a dugout supplied with single or double floats to give it stability; the five-piece canoe, a dugout underbody with two planks sewn on to form the sides, and two others, often elaborately carved, for the bow and stern; and the "lakatois raft," made of several dugouts lashed together and covered with a platform or deck of planks. Both paddles and sails are used for propulsion.

The trade is carried on through an elaborate series of ritual relations established between individuals living in different islands and villages. Under the cover of these ritual partnerships, trading expeditions are enabled to carry on trade even between mutually hostile communities, trading partners being bound to one another by ties of friendship and hospitality. Several island communities may be linked together in such a "kula" relationship, thus forming a "kula ring," a series of communities between which there is a constant exchange of both ritual and economic goods and services. This aspect of Melanesian culture has been excellently described in Bronislaw Malinowski's *Argonauts of the Western Pacific*.[8]

4) Polynesia and Micronesia.—Polynesia and Micronesia are essentially similar to Melanesia in cutting tools and containers. House types, however, are distinctive, the pile dwellings and tree houses of Melanesia and Papua giving way to houses built either on the ground or on stone platforms. Within Polynesia alone there is considerable variation in style of house. In Samoa we find well-made round or oval structures of poles set upon the ground with walls of

---
[8] London, 1922.

mats which can be rolled up. The floor is paved with coral or pebbles and upon it mats are laid for sleeping or reclining. But in the Marquesas the houses are rectangular and much more solidly built, with a heavy framework and solid walls. All such structures rest on stone platforms, the height and area of the platform being symbolic of the family's wealth and prestige. And in New Zealand are found great council houses, measuring 100 by 30 feet, set on the ground. These have a framework of timbers, solid walls, and heavily thatched roofs. Many of them are elaborately decorated with carvings and painted designs.

Like the Melanesians, the Polynesians and Micronesians are fishermen and agriculturalists. The most important crops are coconuts, breadfruit, bananas and other plantains, yams, taro, and the paper mulberry tree. The last-named is cultivated for its bark, which is used in making bark cloth. Polynesian bark cloth is the best to be found anywhere in the world and, before European contact, was the only material of which clothing was made. Clothing is more elaborate in Polynesia than in Melanesia, the men wearing loincloths and the women wrap-around skirts. Robes of bark cloth, feathers, and matting are also found. Scarification is never practiced, but tattooing is widespread.

Fishing in Polynesia and Micronesia is, if anything, more highly developed than in Melanesia. Except in New Zealand, it appears to be the principal source of food, agriculture and domestic animals (pigs and chickens) only supplementing the food obtained from the sea. Many techniques are employed: shellfish are gathered from the reefs and beaches, and other fish are speared, poisoned, or caught with hook and line or nets. Everywhere, fishing is bound up with innumerable rituals and ceremonies, and there is often a group of professional fishermen-priests to enforce the taboos and regulate the ceremonies.

Specialization of labor is highly developed within Polynesian communities, but there is not the same development of village specialization and elaborately ritualized trade that we find in

Melanesia. Contact between communities and islands in Polynesia is most often of a hostile nature and warfare plays an important role in both Polynesian and Micronesian culture.

Sea travel, however, is highly important, and Polynesian and Micronesian boats are as good as, if not better than, those of the Melanesians. The Polynesians especially were inveterate sailors and are known to have made long voyages of exploration, remaining out of sight of land for days and transporting whole communities from one island group to another. Boats are mostly of the five-piece type already described; they are large, well built, and seaworthy, and propelled by paddles and sails. There is considerable knowledge of navigational techniques; in both Polynesia and Micronesia, maps and charts, carved in wood, are used in navigation.

5) *Malaysia.*—The material culture of Malaysia has been much influenced by diffusion from India and China. According to Kroeber,[9] the most profound influence has been exerted by India. Beginning nearly two thousand years ago, Indian adventurers and refugees, centered in Sumatra and Java, brought advanced architectural forms, sculpture, writing, iron, cotton, and many other items of material culture to the less advanced Malays. As a result we find that cutting tools in this area are mainly of iron, stone and bamboo being used only by the more isolated peoples. Clothing is of woven cotton and bark cloth, the loincloth, turban, skirt, and robe being the prevailing articles of dress. Typical weapons are the blowgun, the knife, and the head axe; here, as in most of Oceania, the bow and arrow are conspicuously absent. Containers are usually of pottery and basketry, though bamboo containers are not unknown, especially among the more isolated peoples.

Agriculture is the primary means of obtaining food, and here, too, we may note Asiatic influence in that rice is the staple food. There are in Malaysia two techniques of cultivation: the "dry rice" or dibble technique, and the "wet rice" method. In the former, which is widely distributed among the more backward peoples, the

---

[9] A. L. Kroeber, *Anthropology* (New York, 1923), p. 488.

land is cleared by burning and the kernels of seed rice are dropped into small holes made by a pointed dibble stick. The crop receives some care while growing and is harvested by hand. The latter method, the wet rice technique, is more elaborate: seed beds are prepared and carefully irrigated; fields, too, are flooded, and to them the young rice plants are removed by hand at the proper time. In the mountainous regions of Malaysia terracing is extensively employed to supply adequate space for the growing crop.

In addition to the pig and the chicken, which, as we have seen, are widely distributed in Oceania, the Malaysians have domesticated the water buffalo or carabao. Fishing plays some part in the food quest but does not have the vital role it assumes in Melanesia, Polynesia, and Micronesia. Hunting, throughout Malaysia, is practiced only as a sport.

Water transportation is well developed among the coastal Malays and among the inland peoples living near navigable streams. The boats, though well constructed, are not so large or elaborate as those of the Polynesians, nor are the Malays as enthusiastic or as adventurous seafarers. Indeed, most of the more advanced Malays are fairly sedentary, living in large, permanent villages and towns. Houses are well constructed of wood and thatch, and are often set on piles. Both single-family dwellings and large communal houses are found, the latter often being of great size.

*Social Organization.*—By social organization we refer to the divisions of society—familial, political, economic, and religious—necessary to its integration. Since it will be impossible to describe in detail all the variations of social organization to be found in Oceania, we shall select certain groups, not necessarily the most typical, for brief description. By this means we can gain some notion of the bewildering variety of forms and, at the same time, lay the groundwork for at least a tentative classification of these forms.

1) *Australia.*—In Australia and Tasmania, as well as among most of the Negrito peoples of Malaysia, we find a simple form of social organization resting almost wholly on the tie of kinship. Notable

among these groups is the almost complete absence of any political institution:[10] there are no political groupings, or, at best, only temporary ones; no chiefs, no systems of codified law or courts to administer them; nor are there any clearly defined economic or religious institutions. All the functions performed by these—the maintenance of social order, the distribution of goods, and the maintenance of relations with the supernatural—are performed by the familial institution.

The structure of the family and other social units based upon kinship is not the same, however, in all these societies. Here we shall describe only Australian social organization, but it must not be assumed that this is typical of the entire group. Data is lacking on the social organization of the Tasmanians, but the Negrito social forms are well delineated in A. R. Radcliffe Brown's *The Andaman Islanders*,[11] to which the reader is referred for a picture contrasting in many details with that of Australia.

In Australia generally, according to Radcliffe Brown,[12] there are four basic units of social organization:

*a*) The family, consisting of a man, his wife, and their children. This group shares a dwelling place. Marriage is always monogamous, though either the man or the woman can break up the marriage and marry again. The family never exists in isolation; it always forms part of a larger unit.

*b*) The horde or band, a small group of interrelated families occupying a definite territory or hunting ground. Proprietary rights to this territory are held in common; trespass by members of another band is cause for war. Membership in the band is determined by birth, the children belonging to their father's band. Men never leave the band of their birth, but women leave theirs at marriage for their husband's band. The band is politically and economically

---

[10] The term "institution" is being used here in the sense defined by Chapple and Coon, *op. cit.*, p. 287.

[11] London, 1933.

[12] A. R. Radcliffe Brown, *The Social Organization of Australian Tribes* (Oceania Monographs, No. 1; London, 1931).

independent and is ruled by an informal council consisting of the older men of the band. These men, however, are related as "fathers" or "grandfathers" to all the people in the horde and rule by virtue of this relationship, not by virtue of any extrakinship authority.

*c*) Crosscutting the division into bands, there is, within any "tribe" (see *d,* below), a division into groupings based on sex and age. In some tribes there are two such groupings (which are then called "moieties"), in others four ("sections"), and in still others eight ("subsections"). Membership in all such groups is by birth. In the moiety system, a child may belong, in some tribes, to his mother's moiety; in others, to his father's. He must marry into a moiety not his own. Where the tribe is divided into four sections, the child belongs, not to his father's or mother's section, but to a third section, and he must find a spouse in the fourth section. Where the eight-subsection system is followed, the child belongs to the subsection of his paternal grandfather and takes a spouse from the subsection of his paternal grandmother. If the child is a male, his children will belong to his father's subsection, but if a female, her children will belong to the subsection of her husband's father.

*d*) The tribe, composed of a group of bands speaking the same or closely related dialects. This is in no sense a political entity; members of different hordes of the same tribe recognize one another as friends only if a kinship tie can be established between them.

It is evident, then, that an Australian aborigine recognizes only one binding tie—that of kinship. Ordinarily he has contacts only with those with whom he is related; during the aboriginal period, a person who wandered into a territory occupied by persons with whom he had no ties of kinship would have been killed. All relations between individuals, whether economic, political, affinal, or otherwise, are guided in terms of an elaborate system of duties and privileges attendant upon the kinship tie. Since, in Australia, the widest possible recognition is given to genealogical relationship, and since these relationships are made the basis of an extensive and highly organized system of reciprocal obligations, it is clear that "the question of genealogical relationship ... regulates more or less definitely the behavior of an individual to every person with whom he has any social dealings whatsoever."[13]

The religion of the Australian has often been referred to as "totemism" and, like all other social activities, is clearly bound up with the kinship group. It is believed by the Australians that they were preceded by an ancestral people who lived in the mythological past. When these people died, their bodies passed into the earth and the spot was marked with a tree or stone. Their fetishes, objects of stone or wood marked with designs, were left behind and are collected by the present-day people and stored near the sacred spots where the bodies of the ancestors disappeared. The souls of the ancestors split into two; one soul remained with the fetish and the other remained in the sacred spot seeking to enter the body of a living woman and be reborn as a human being. Therefore, everyone born is the reincarnation of an ancestral spirit and, since his twin soul dwells in a fetish stored at the sacred spot from which his soul emerged, he has a mystical relationship with that sacred place. All those having mystical relations with the same sacred spot belong to the same totem group.

Within the territory of a band there may be several sacred spots or totem centers. Each is mystically connected with a natural species—an animal, insect, plant, or other natural object. Since, as we have described, each totem center is bound to a group of human beings, a mystical relationship is believed to exist between the natural species, the totem center, the mythological ancestors, and a group of humans. The humans perform rites, sometimes localized at the totem center and sometimes not, for the increase of the natural species to which they are bound. One of the group acts as leader in the performance of these rites.

The totem group, then, forms another subdivision of the band based upon kinship, though here the kinship is strengthened by supernatural sanctions. By this means the living individual is linked

---
[13] *Ibid.*, p. 12.

as kin to his ancestors and, directly or indirectly, to the natural species significant in his economic life. When he dies, his soul returns to the totem center, eventually to be reborn into the world as a human being.

2) The Papuans of New Guinea.—Among the Papuans of New Guinea, as among the Australians, it is amply evident that kinship rather than political groupings plays a dominant role in social organization. Thus, according to Margaret Mead,[14] "the lack of any form of political organization capable of integrating more than a few hundred people is... conspicuous for this area. The typical picture is a cluster of hamlets, bound together by ties of intermarriage, ceremonial coöperation and perhaps coöperation in headhunting raids.... The entire region depends upon kinship ties as the major social mechanism."

The forms taken by Papuan social groupings, however, are by no means identical with, or indeed very similar to, those of Australia. Briefly, Papuan social groups comprise the primary family, the clan or extended family, the village or "cluster of hamlets," and, in some places, loosely organized warmaking groups of three to four villages.

The Papuan family consists of a man, his wife or wives, and their children. Polygyny is fairly generally permitted, though not everywhere extensively practiced. Residence is patrilocal, the wife coming to live in her husband's village. This group occupies a single dwelling or, sometimes, a part of a communal dwelling.

Far more important in Papuan social organization is the extended family or clan. Two forms are distinguished: patrilineal clans, which include all individuals related in the male line; and matrilineal clans, where relationship is reckoned through the mother. The dominant pattern seems to be one of localized patrilineal clans; that is, a system whereby the people of a given hamlet or even village are all related through the male line and form a more or

---

[14] *The Mountain Arapesh* (American Museum of Natural History, Anthropological Papers, Vol. XXXVI, Part III, 1938), p. 160.

less autonomous group. A further division of the community into halves or moieties is also widespread. Both the clan division and the moiety division may be reflected in the physical arrangement of the houses in the village. Thus, Thurnwald reports for the Bánaro: "The external form of the settlement reflects precisely the internal organization of the tribe; for the goblin-hall [i.e., a ceremonial house], with adjacent houses in the same clearing, mirrors the social unit, the gens [i.e., our "clan"], just as the symmetric partition of the goblin-hall into two parts, the division of the gens into halves."[15]

The clan exercises control over all its members by reason of their relationship to one another. It also regulates marriage, since one must always find a spouse outside one's clan. Ceremonial and ritual activities are similarly guided by clan membership. Strikingly characteristic of Papuan social life are the competitive and reciprocal exchanges of pigs and other articles of value between persons of different clans. According to Stirling: "The object of these competitions is to 'break' the individual in whose 'honor' the feast is given, as he is obliged by custom to return the compliment even more elaborately. Clan members contribute to the cause of their respective representatives, and great social prestige is acquired by the victor. The loser, on the other hand, is doomed to disgrace and poverty, and the clans share in the glory or disgrace, as the case might be."[16]

As we have said, the village in Papua consists of one or more hamlets, each of which is composed of a group of related individuals, usually through the male line. The hamlets comprising a village are bound together by ties of kinship and marriage, and may coöperate in ceremonial observances and in warfare. The village is not, however, a fully developed political entity; there is rarely any form of institutionalized leadership, nor is there a centralized system for the regulation of the behavior of its members. Indeed, there is no mechanism whereby the allegiance of the hamlet or

[15] Richard Thurnwald, *Bánaro Society,* as reprinted in A. L. Kroeber and T. T. Waterman, *Source Book in Anthropology* (New York, 1931), p. 285.
[16] M. W. Stirling, *The Native Peoples of New Guinea* (Smithsonian Institution, War Background Studies, No. 9, 1943), p. 21.

kinship group to the village can be retained; any of the constituent groups of the village may form other ties whenever it likes. In summary, then, the Papuan village is a weakly organized group of extended families or clans held together solely by ties of kinship. A village may persist over a long period of time and the constant association of its members in coöperative activity may lead to the formation of a simple political institution with the leadership vested in one or more individuals who have acquired position and prestige in the community. Such positions, however, are not hereditary, and the political order founded by an individual falls apart at his death.

The larger federations of three or four villages are even less integrated. Essentially, these exist only for the purpose of waging war against a common enemy, and once this function has been achieved the temporary union ceases to exist. Needless to say, such occasional alliances of villages for purposes of warfare do not preclude the possibility of war, later, between the erstwhile allies, and the consequent organization of other alliances of quite a different constituency.

As we have indicated earlier, trade is important between Papuan villages. In some regions there is considerable specialization in the production of foodstuffs with a consequent exchange of specialties between villages. In general, this trade is carried on by means of gift exchanges; often the competitive feasts referred to above serve as a primary means of distributing such goods.

Totemism, broadly similar to that found in Australia, is also characteristic of some Papuan tribes. Here, however, the totem group is identical with the clan, all of whose members are believed to be descended from an ancestor common to both men and a natural species. There are, however, no ceremonies for the increase of the natural species, nor is the concept of a localized totem center a part of the belief.

More important in the ritual life are puberty ceremonies for boys. In these, boys are carried off into the bush, kept from certain foods and subjected to other restrictions upon their behavior, circumcized, and finally put through a series of ceremonies intended to initiate them into the secrets of adult life. Such ceremonies are conducted by men and are kept a secret from the women, who characteristically play little part in ritual activity.

3) The Melanesians.—Among the Australians and Papuans we noted that kinship ties functioned as the major social mechanisms, though in Papua there was at least a rudimentary political institution standing over and above the social units based upon kin. In Melanesia the political institution is somewhat more advanced than in Papua, though still short of the complexity to be found among the Polynesians.

As among the Papuans, however, we find in Melanesia that the primary and extended family units are responsible for a large part of the maintenance of social order. Marriage may be monogamous or polygynous, though monogamy is the prevailing form. Members of the primary family live together in a single house, less often occupying space in a communal dwelling. The extended family is usually patrilineal, sometimes matrilineal, and, less often, bilateral. Such units, however they may be constituted, often live in a part of the village, own land in common, and cultivate it coöperatively. In some areas, however, the extended families are not localized but may be found in several quite distinct political groupings or villages. The extended family is always exogamous; that is, a man must find his spouse outside his family unit.

Cutting across familial lines are a number of men's associations, variously designated as sections, men's societies, or secret societies. Each of these has a distinctive name, owns a large canoe, and centers its activities in a men's house. Many of its activities are ritualistic, but each section has certain duties in the collection and preparation of food for feasts, in the building of canoes and canoe houses, and in fishing. The names of the sections, which usually refer to warlike activities, suggest that these groups may formerly have functioned also as fighting units. A man apparently selects his own section and usually selects the one in which his relatives are numerous. In some regions, and perhaps in all, both sections and extended families are subject to an informal grading whereby the society as a whole is divided into "noble" families and sections and "commoner" families and sections. These class lines, however, are not too rigidly drawn; it is quite possible that a family or section may change its classification in the course of years.

A third division of Melanesian society may be described as political. Here we find the unit to be the village or, perhaps oftener, several villages united by a common allegiance to a chiefly or "noble" family. One member of this family, always a man, is regarded as the leader or chief and is accorded a certain deference by virtue of his position. He may also receive gifts from the peoples under his control for his support, but these are never sufficient for his needs. The house occupied by the chiefly family is the largest in the village and is usually elaborately decorated. Since it is built by communal effort it belongs to the village or confederation of villages and may be used as a place of assembly as well as the chief's dwelling. The chieftainship is hereditary, the office descending to the nearest male relative who is a member of the chief's extended family.

We have already mentioned the intensive trading between autonomous political units that is so characteristic of Melanesian society. This trade, it was pointed out, depends upon the existence of ritual partnerships between individuals of differing political groupings, and results in the formation of kula rings uniting several distinct villages or groups of villages into exclusive trading groups. Such trading groups, however, do not take on a political structure; the ties that hold them together are exclusively economic and ritual. Indeed, warfare may occur between villages belonging to the same kula ring; in short, the ritual and trading relationships of a village or confederation of villages do not disturb its political autonomy, nor do they necessarily result in the formation of larger political units.

Religion and ritual in Melanesia is very like that of Papua. Totemism is found, though it is less important than in Papua. Similarly, puberty ceremonies are, in Melanesia, conducted for both boys and girls; there is not the same exclusion of women from ritual activity that we found among the Papuans. Ritual activities are, however, largely in the hands of the men's association and are concerned with the placating of ghosts and spirits, as well as with the exercise of magic and witchcraft. In both Melanesia and Papua, it may be added, illness and misfortune are believed to be caused by sorcery. Much of the ceremonial and ritual activity, therefore, is devoted to protecting the individual and the group from the evil magic of its enemies, and to attacking one's enemies by means of such supernatural powers. In neither region is there any organized priesthood nor any clearly defined hierarchy of gods.

4) *Polynesia and Micronesia.*—Polynesian social and political organization differs quite widely in detail as one moves from Hawaii in the north to New Zealand in the south. In spite of this wide variation within the area, however, there are certain features common to all Polynesia—and shared to some extent by Micronesia—which set it off from the other places. We shall, then, concentrate our attention on these distinctively Polynesian traits of social organization and ignore, for the most part, the numerous variants within the Polynesian area.

Micronesia is too little known to be discussed in detail. Broadly speaking, it appears to share certain of the characteristic elements of Polynesian social organization, such as mana, taboo, powerful, aristocratic, and sacred chiefs, and rigid social stratification dependent upon birth. It differs from Polynesia in possessing throughout exogamous matrilineal clans and in the general prevalence of monogamous marriages. In general, the regions of Micronesia nearest Polynesia are closer to it in culture; as one moves farther away, there are more differences with Polynesia.

Throughout Polynesia the smallest unit of social organization is the household group; that is, a group of blood or affinal kin who occupy the same or adjacent dwellings. The precise composition of this group varies widely. Thus, in the Marquesas the typical household unit consists of a young man who has the highest rank and is therefore the head, his wife or wives, and the subsidiary husbands of his wife or wives. Sometimes a woman is the head of the household; then the remaining adult members are her husbands, one of whom is designated as the principal husband. All the men of the household have conjugal rights over the women; the head has the power of regulating and dispensing these rights. Other members of the household might include older male and female relatives of the head and the children born to the women of the household. The oldest child of the principal wife becomes head as soon as born; the adult head, however, acts as regent until the child is old enough to marry and assume the responsibilities of headship. When the heir marries, the adults of his parents' generation either remain in the household in a subordinate capacity or, if they are still young enough, join another household in the capacity of secondary spouse. The other children born in the household remain only until maturity, when they go to another household as principal or secondary wives (if female) or as secondary husbands (if male). A young male, not the oldest child in his household, can, in theory, establish another household, with himself as head; usually, however, he lacks the resources in wealth and labor to accomplish this end.

The Samoan household is perhaps more typical of Polynesia as a whole. Here is found a unit which may number as many as fifty individuals, who occupy adjoining houses, and who are related to one another by blood, adoption, or marriage. In each of the houses lives a man, his wife (monogamy prevails except among the highest chiefs), and their children, either actual or adopted. All the members of the household acknowledge the authority of the head, always an older man who holds a title of some kind. He is treated with respect, performs the ritual duties of the household, and has, in theory, absolute control over the land and over the lives of the members of the household. Actually, however, his authority may be disputed, and if he becomes unpopular by reason of arbitrary or cruel behavior he may be deposed. Marriage must be with an individual who is not closely related in either the paternal or maternal lines. It is often preceded, for both boys and girls, by a period of promiscuity, one of the trials at living together usually leading to a permanent union. The daughters of powerful chiefs excepted, virginity is not required of the bride.

Household groups throughout Polynesia are combined into villages, which are often the primary political units. Sometimes the political unit is the tribe, made up of more than one village and numbering as many as 1,200 individuals. Strong kingdoms with highly centralized governments were found only in Hawaii and New Zealand, though in some islands, like the Marquesas, tribes would occasionally band together in temporary confederacies for purposes of warfare and feasting.

The Polynesian political grouping is ruled by a chief, aided by a council consisting of household heads, priests, outstanding warriors, and other men of rank. In theory, the chief is an absolute ruler holding all political power; in actual practice, his decisions and rulings are controlled by public opinion expressed through the tribal council. In some regions, such as the Marquesas, a chief who becomes unpopular may be abandoned by his subjects.

Chieftainship is hereditary in Polynesia and the position goes to the individual of the tribe who possesses the greatest amount of mana. Mana is conceived as impersonal supernatural power, which can reside in human beings, natural phenomena, images, gods, and many other things both animate and inanimate. The test of its presence is the efficiency and power of the person or thing which possesses it; a successful fisherman is believed to have mana, but if his luck changes he has lost his mana. Chiefs rule by virtue of their mana, which is correlated with descent. The more directly one is descended from the common ancestor of the tribe, the greater one's mana. Consequently, individuals in a tribe are ranked according to their mana, the greatest being found in the head chief, less in the heads of noble families, and least in the lowest commoners.

Slaves have no mana; thus, a chief who is captured and made a slave loses his mana by virtue of this occurrence.

One result of this belief is a stratification of Polynesian society as follows:

*a*) Slaves. Individuals who have no rights, no mana, and no social standing. They are usually attached to certain families as servitors and retainers.

*b*) Free commoners. There are several subclasses of commoners, depending upon birth and occupation. Thus, canoe builders, fishermen, and certain other skilled artisans, including warriors, are of the uppermost strata, whereas those without special skills are of the lowest class of commoners, only slightly above slaves.

*c*) *Metapules.* In some Polynesian societies, particularly in Tonga and the Society Islands, we find this class, intermediate between the commoner and the chiefly classes. *Metapules* are the personal servitors of the king or supreme chief. Since the king possesses great mana and since this possession can be lost by contact with members of his own group lower than himself in the social scale, his servants, who are always foreigners and therefore nonconductors of mana, are the only ones who can personally attend the king. This position of easy access to the king, of course, gives them much influence.

*d*) Priests. Priests vary in rank. In some communities the high priest outranks the king when possessed by the god he symbolizes. In others, priests are just a higher class of commoner, occupying the highest position by virtue of their profession and access to the gods.

*e*) Chiefs. These form the highest class and are graded according to their position of leadership, from the rulers of villages to the supreme chief of a tribe. The supreme chief, of course, has a great deal of mana and often for this reason is unable to come in contact with commoners. As a result we find the development of dual chieftainship. Thus, in Samoa, there are hereditary chiefs who are helpless to rule and who function only as sources of authority. Actual rulership is vested in the "talking" or "speaker" chiefs, generally commoners, who are elected by the villages.

Correlated with the concept of mana is that of taboo. A thing taboo is a thing to be avoided. Certain holy places, images, chiefs, and priests, because of their great mana, are under constant taboo: no one of lesser rank can touch them or anything that has come in contact with them. Thus, in New Zealand the chief cannot go out in the daytime lest his shadow fall upon commoners and cause their death. His old clothes are destroyed, his house is poor, he has no servants, and no one can come near him. He cannot enter the house of a commoner, for everything that passes over his head must at once be destroyed.

Temporary taboos can be put upon various things for specific purposes. Thus, a king can taboo cattle killing for a period to increase the herds, or he can taboo the collection of crops to save them for a particular occasion. He can similarly taboo a village to punish its occupants; during the taboo no one can leave or enter the village. Similar taboos can be imposed by owners upon their property to keep it from being stolen or used during their absence. Needless to say, the efficacy of a taboo depends upon the mana of the one who imposes it; the taboo is only effective against those who have less mana than the one who imposes the taboo.

In Polynesia, ritual activity, like most other activities, is highly specialized. Everywhere we find a pantheon of gods, ranked much as are their human descendants on earth. Priests are often of two classes: inspirational priests, who are believed to be possessed, at appropriate intervals, by a particular god and, while so possessed, to speak with the voice and authority of the god himself; and ritual priests, who are specialists in one or other of the numerous rituals necessary to the proper conduct of life. Inspirational priests rank highest and, within this class of priests, in accordance with the importance of the god who possesses them. It is noteworthy, however, that an important god only inspires men of high rank; a person of no importance who claims the inspiration of a god of high rank will not be believed. Ritual priests are usually master craftsmen, specialists in the ritual of a trade as well as in the trade itself. They too are ranked, in accordance with the importance of their craft. Both craft and ritual are learned through a long apprenticeship; the reward comes from the prestige of position and the monetary returns the skill commands.

5) Malaysia.—With respect to social and political organization three quite distinctive cultural patterns may be noted in Malaysia. First, we find the Negritos, who are organized primarily along lines of kinship, with only a temporary political institution in the village or band. Second, there is the fundamental Malay pattern, varying somewhat from region to region but based primarily on the bilateral family, the village governed by an elected chief and village council, and the absence of strongly drawn class lines. Certain tribes of Sumatra, notably the Menang Kabau, differ most markedly from this general pattern in the possession of strongly developed matrilineal clans. Third and last, there are the complex kingdoms of Java, Bali, and certain other islands of the Sunda group which are a result of conquest and immigration from India. This influence, according to Kroeber, "introduced architecture, sculpture, writing, monarchy, religion, iron, cotton, and a host of other elements of higher culture. The earlier Indian influence was Buddhist and its seat of power centered in southern Sumatra; the later was Brahmin and reached its zenith in Java. The number of immigrants was probably small, their effect enormous. A group of refugees, ... would found a colony, sometimes conquering the natives, sometimes attaching them peacefully to their leadership, and soon a little kingdom was flourishing, which in time sent out other offshoots or absorbed its rivals until its name commanded respect and tribute for long distances across the sea."[17]

Since the Negritos are clearly outside the Malaysian cultural tradition and the higher civilizations of the Sunda Islands just as obviously intrusive, we shall concentrate our attention on what we

[17] A. L. Kroeber, *Anthropology*, p. 488.

have called the fundamental Malay pattern. Thus, among the Dyaks of Borneo, who fairly well illustrate this pattern, we find that the tribe is not a centrally organized political unit but merely a group of people living in the same territory who share similar customs and speak dialects of the same language. Warfare might occur between members of the same tribe, but this is rare; even though no political ties unite them, the members of a single tribe are felt to be friendly. The functioning governmental unit is the village, made up of from one to six communal dwellings. Each of these "long houses" has its own chief; when a village comprises several long houses, one of the house chiefs is also the village chief. Chieftainship is informally elective, but the chief must be from the so-called "aristocracy" and there is a tendency to give the position to the son of a former chief. The chief is not paid for his services, though he receives many gifts from his people and derives considerable social prestige from his position.

Chiefs, their families, and their relatives form an aristocratic class within the community. Below these are the commoners, free people holding property. Many of this class are skilled artisans. Lowest of all are the war captives, who are attached to certain "noble" families, have no status in marriage or ceremonial, and do not usually hold property. Class lines are, however, none too clear, and the class affiliation of a given family might easily be changed. Marriage is normally with a person of the same class, but here again class lines can be crossed.

Monogamy is the general rule in marriage, though chiefs often have more than one wife. Marriage is usually preceded by a period of promiscuity or "trial marriage," one such temporary union usually terminating in permanent marriage. Such casual liaisons are made easy by the fact that the boys and girls of the village live in the boys' house and girls' house, respectively, and not in the same house as their parents. After marriage, a young couple start a new household, receive a room in the long house, and a section of the village lands for cultivation.

Religion and ritual in Malaysia is subject to the same wide variation as that we have noted in social organization. On the one hand, we find the simple unorganized religious and ritual activity of the Negitos; on the other, the complexities of the Indian rituals of Java, Bali, and others of the Sunda Islands. Basic throughout the region, however, are the Malay beliefs and practices. Here, as in Melanesia, there is no organized priesthood and few elaborate ceremonies. Usually, the practitioner or shaman is an individual who makes his living as everyone else does but, because of special powers, gains a measure of contact with the supernatural.

Thus, among the Tinguian of northern Luzon the shaman or medium is almost always a woman past the age of childbearing. Fits of trembling or warnings in dreams notify her that she has been selected by the spirits as a medium of communication to her fellows. She then goes to an older medium to learn the detailed techniques of her craft, a training which may last for several months. Mediums are necessary for the performance of all ceremonies; most of these have to do with the placation of evil spirits and the securing of benefits, in health and wealth, for the participants.

*Summary and Conclusions.*—It is clear from what has been said in the preceding pages that Oceania—racially, linguistically, and culturally—may broadly be divided into two great subareas. The first of these—Australia and Tasmania—is distinguished from the second—Malaysia, Melanesia, Micronesia, and Polynesia—primarily by its isolation. As a result of geographical isolation from both Asia and the islands of the southwest Pacific, the aboriginal peoples and cultures of Australia and Tasmania developed very slowly and along unique lines. It is probably not too much to say that the racial, cultural, and linguistic phenomena found within this territory have little or no traceable historical connection with others anywhere in the world.

Today the aborigines of Australia and Tasmania play no significant role in the modern civilization of this region. The Tasmanians, as we have seen, became extinct at an early date—so soon after

European contact that we have little or no adequate data on their languages and cultures. The Australians, living in small and widely scattered bands, were soon rendered impotent. Today they live, like our North American Indians, on reservations. Except for a few borrowings of words and place names, modern Australian culture has not been influenced in the slightest by that of the aborigines.

In the rest of Oceania there is a clearly traceable historical connection between southeastern Asia, Malaysia, Melanesia, Micronesia, and Polynesia. This connection is best evidenced on the side of race or physical type: throughout the island region there is a greater or less admixture of southern Mongoloid blood, connecting the inhabitants with those of southeastern Asia, and here and there clear evidences of an archaic Mediterranean Caucasoid strain, ultimately bound up, probably, with the Mediterranean Caucasoid inhabitants of India. Culturally, Malaysia shows most clearly the influences of the great Asiatic culture centers; this influence rapidly thins out as one moves north and east from the Sunda Islands. In language, there is little to tie Oceania to the Asiatic mainland; as yet, only the isolated Mon Khmer languages of Oceania have any clear relationship to Asiatic language groups.

Though many details are still lacking, it appears clear that the islands were populated by a series of slow movements of peoples of diverse racial and cultural origins from the mainland to and throughout the island area. Dating is uncertain, but it may be said that the advance to the islands probably did not begin until the Neolithic was well under way, certainly less than ten thousand years ago.

The island cultures of today, unlike those of Australia and Tasmania, have not everywhere been completely submerged by European contact. Indeed, in the regions difficult of access by reason of climate and terrain the aboriginal civilizations are still relatively untouched. Thus, Stirling reports: "The interior of New Guinea is today the last real stronghold of the stone age existing in the world. The much-abused expression 'have never seen a white man' is literally true for many thousands of the interior natives of New Guinea. As late as 1926 when the writer explored the Nassau Mountains by way of the Mamberamo River, it was found that the natives of the Van Rees and Gautier Mountains of the northern coast range had but few objects of metal. When we reached the great interior lake plain, the Papuans of the western half of this area knew nothing whatever of metals or any other product of the white man, nor did the pigmy tribes of the central mountains."[18]

In other portions of Oceania, however, European culture has made great progress. The Hawaiians and the Maori (of New Zealand), for example, have assimilated fairly completely to European ways of life. Weckler points out that Polynesians living in port cities "are largely 'detribalized,' have given up most of their Polynesian ways and have become a landless proletariat," and that "the Hawaiians have for the most part accepted the American way of political and economic life and take their part in Hawaiian affairs pretty much on a par with the other racial and cultural groups of those islands."[19] Similarly, "the Maori have developed in recent years, along with a remarkable renaissance of traditional literature and legend, tribal community life, native games, dancing and music, etiquette and ceremony, methods of coöperative farming and ranching on their own lands. Coöperative ownership and work fit in very well with the customary Polynesian methods of getting jobs done, and the enterprises operate successfully at lower costs than small nonnative holders can manage. It is possible that Polynesians on other islands might enter world economy successfully in the future through the development of coöperative production operated by and for themselves."[20]

Throughout the vast island region of Oceania, then, there has been, as a result of European and American exploration, exploitation, and control, a greater or less modification of the aboriginal cul-

---

[18] M. W. Stirling, *op. cit.*, p. 11.
[19] J. E. Weckler, Jr., *Polynesians, Explorers of the Pacific* (Smithsonian Institution, War Background Studies, No. 6, 1943), p. 59.
[20] *Ibid.*

tures by the introduction of European things and ideas. In few places, however, has the substratum of aboriginal culture been entirely lost. As a result, island Oceania is today a region of mixed cultures. Since Europeans, Americans, or Asiatics everywhere dominate the political and economic life, the native peoples are political minorities, usually denied equal access to the benefits of the new civilization. Problems of interracial and intercultural relations are many and their solution vital to the establishment of peaceful and progressive community life. It is only by patient and long-continued study, of the earlier native civilizations as well as those of the modern island communities, that solutions to these problems will be found.

## SELECTED BIBLIOGRAPHY

### Australia and Tasmania

A. W. Howitt, *The Native Tribes of Southeast Australia*, London, 1914.
G. P. Murdock, *Our Primitive Contemporaries*, New York, 1934, pp. 1–19, 20–47.
A. R. Radcliffe Brown, *The Social Organization of Australian Tribes* (Oceania Monographs, No. 1), London, 1931.
B. Spencer and F. J. Gillen, *The Northern Tribes of Central Australia*, London, 1904.
———, *The Native Tribes of Central Australia*, London, 1899.
———, *The Arunta*, London, 1927; 2 vols.
W. Lloyd Warner, *A Black Civilization*, New York, 1937.
H. L. Roth, *The Aborigines of Tasmania*, London, 1890.

### Malaysia

R. F. Barton, *The Half Way Sun*, New York, 1930.
———, *Ifugao Economics* (University of California Publications in American Archaeology and Ethnology, Vol. 15, No. 5), Berkeley, 1919.
———, *Ifugao Law* (University of California Publications in American Archaeology and Ethnology, Vol. 15, No. 1), Berkeley, 1919.
A. R. Radcliffe Brown, *The Andaman Islanders*, Cambridge, 1933.
Donald Campbell, *Java: Past and Present*, London, 1915; 2 vols.
Fay-Cooper Cole, *The Tinguian* (Field Museum of Natural History), Chicago, 1915.
———, *Wild Tribes of Davao District, Mindanoa* (Field Museum of Natural History), Chicago, 1913.
Miguel Covarrubias, *Island of Bali*, New York, 1937.
C. Hose and Wm. MacDougall, *The Pagan Tribes of Borneo*, London, 1912; 2 vols.
A. E. Jenks, *The Bontoc Igorot*, Manila, 1905.
Carl Lumholz, *Through Central Borneo*, New York, 1920; 2 vols.
W. W. Skeat, *Malay Magic*, London, 1900.
George Whitehead, *In the Nicobar Islands*, 1924.

### Melanesia

Beatrice Blackwood, *Both Sides of Buka Passage*, Oxford, 1935.
George Brown, *Melanesians and Polynesians*, London, 1910.
R. H. Codrington, *The Melanesians*, Oxford, 1891.
R. F. Fortune, *The Sorcerers of Dobu*, New York, 1932.
W. G. Ivens, *Melanesians of the Southeast Solomon Islands*, London, 1927.
Gunnar Landtmann, *The Kiwai Papuans of British New Guinea*, New York, 1927.
Bronislaw Malinowski, *The Argonauts of the Western Pacific*, London, 1922.
———, *The Sexual Life of Savages*, London, 1929.
———, *Coral Gardens and Their Magic*, London, 1935.
Margaret Mead, *The Mountain Arapesh* (American Museum of Natural History, Anthropological Papers, Vol. XXXVI, Part III), Washington, D. C., 1938.
———, *Growing Up in New Guinea*, 1930.

## 68    The Southwest Pacific and the War

H. Powdermaker, *Life in Lesu*, New York, 1933.
W. H. R. Rivers, *The History of Melanesian Society*, Cambridge, 1914; 2 vols.
C. G. Seligman, *The Melanesians of British Guinea*, Cambridge, 1910.
M. W. Stirling, *The Native Peoples of New Guinea* (Smithsonian Institution, War Background Studies, No. 9), Washington, D.C., 1943.

### POLYNESIA

Ernest and Pearl Beaglehole, *Ethnology of Pukapuka* (Bernice P. Bishop Museum, Bulletin 150), Honolulu, 1938.
Elsdon Best, *The Maori*, New Zealand, 1924.
Peter H. Buck, *The Vikings of the Sunrise*, New York, 1938.
William Ellis, *Polynesian Researches*, London, 1831.
Raymond Firth, *Primitive Polynesian Economy*, London, 1939.
———, *Primitive Economics of the New Zealand Maori*, New York, 1929.
———, *We the Tikopia*, New York, 1936.
E. S. C. Handy, *Native Culture in the Marquesas* (Bernice P. Bishop Museum, Bulletin 9), Honolulu, 1923.
E. S. C. Handy and others, *Ancient Hawaiian Civilization*, Honolulu, 1935.
H. Ian Hogbin, *Law and Order in Polynesia*, New York, 1934.
F. M. Keesing, *The South Seas in the Modern World*, New York, 1941.
Margaret Mead, *Coming of Age in Samoa*, New York, 1936.
Herman Melville, *Typee: Romance of the South Seas*, New York, 1907.
Alfred Métraux, *Easter Island* (Bernice P. Bishop Museum, Bulletin 160), Honolulu, 1940.
I. L. G. Sutherland (ed.), *The Maori People Today*, Wellington, New Zealand, 1940.
G. Turner, *Samoa a Hundred Years Ago and Long Before*, London, 1884.
R. W. Williamson, *The Social and Political Systems of Central Polynesia*, Cambridge, 1924.
———, *Religions and Cosmic Beliefs of Central Polynesia*, Cambridge, 1933.

### MICRONESIA

F. W. Christian, *The Caroline Islands*, 1899.
P. A. Erdland, *Die Marshall-Insulaner*, 1914.
A. Matsumura, *Contributions to the Ethnography of Micronesia*, 1918.
N. Yamazaki, *Micronesia and Micronesians*, 1927.
Tadao Yanaihara, *Pacific Islands under Japanese Mandate*, New York, 1940.

# THE ENTRY OF THE SOUTHWEST PACIFIC INTO WORLD POLITICS

CHARLES L. MOWAT

ASSISTANT PROFESSOR OF HISTORY
IN THE UNIVERSITY OF CALIFORNIA

*Lecture delivered April 12, 1943*

# THE ENTRY OF THE SOUTHWEST PACIFIC INTO WORLD POLITICS

From earliest times the people of Europe have turned their eyes to the East, and have been strangely fascinated by tales of the Spice Islands and Cathay, by

> the wealth of Ormus and of Ind,
> Or where the gorgeous East with richest hand
> Showers on her kings barbaric pearl and gold.

Solomon "made a navy of ships... on the shore of the Red Sea... And they came to Ophir, and fetched from thence gold... [and] great plenty of almug trees, and precious stones." The Solomon Islands, indeed, brought into unhappy prominence by the anguish of our day, were so named in 1567 in anticipation of their natural riches. Yet of all the Orient, indeed of all the world, the South Sea—or the southwest Pacific—remained the latest *mare incognitum;* it is only within the span of many still living that all its archipelagoes have been charted and its islands annexed by one or other of the major powers. Parts of New Guinea remain still unexplored. Not till after the historic voyage of Captain Cook in 1769 was interest or knowledge of the South Seas in any sense popular. Robert Louis Stevenson's residence in Samoa brought further attention to the islands in the late nineteenth century; and in our own day Nordhoff and Hall's account of the mutiny on H.M.S. *Bounty* and their essays on the idyllic life of the South Sea Islands have brought to a wider public a romantic interest in this quarter of the globe. For those seeking to escape the *Sturm und Drang* of the 1920's a coral atoll beside its lagoon in the South Seas, visited perhaps once a year by a sailing vessel trading in copra and canned goods, became the longed-for asylum; for the more sophisticated, wishing only for a temporary retreat, and that with all the modern comforts, there was always Tahiti, or Bali in the Netherlands Indies. In one of the most plaintive blues songs of the period we were all "crying for the Carolines"—a phrase of bitterest irony today.

## 72  The Southwest Pacific and the War

The attraction of these faëry lands forlorn has, as Bernard DeVoto recently pointed out, been dimmed forever by the sufferings of our fighting men in the southwest Pacific.

But though general knowledge of this area may have been long in coming, adventurers, traders, and diplomats have been actively concerned with the East Indies since the sixteenth century, and they, together with missionaries and planters, busily divided Oceania and the rest of this ill-defined area, the southwest Pacific, in the nineteenth century, especially in its last two decades. Annexation, partition, and the bringing of 'civilization' into these parts have been the work of the British, the Dutch, the Spaniards, the Portuguese, the French, the Americans, and for a time the Germans, all acting frequently less from a direct interest in the islands themselves than under the pressures of international, and particularly European, diplomacy, and the imperial rivalries of the last century which sometimes correlated a dispute over the possession of several thousand square miles of African jungle with the ownership of some Pacific archipelago.

It is the political and diplomatic history of this process, extending from the sixteenth century to the twentieth, that is the principal theme of this lecture.[1]

It was in the heroic age of European expansion, the age of discovery, in the fifteenth and sixteenth centuries, that the Pacific was first visited by Westerners and became at once the scene of competing imperialisms. Entry was made by both of the possible routes in less than a generation, and both times by men of Portugal. Diaz rounded the Cape of Good Hope in 1488; Vasco da Gama reached India by that route ten years later. In 1519 Magellan entered the

[1] A summary survey such as this obviously makes no claim to being based on independent research. I have used, in addition to the various secondary works cited later, the standard books of reference, such as the *Dominions Office and Colonial Office List for 1937* (Great Britain), *Whitaker's Almanack*, and the *Encyclopaedia Britannica*. There is no single work surveying the history of the whole of the southwest Pacific; the nearest approach to one is Guy H. Scholefield, *The Pacific, Its Past and Future* (London, 1919), to which I am very heavily indebted. I also owe much to Professor M. W. Graham for valuable advice and suggestions made in the course of preparation of this paper.

Pacific by sailing westward from Europe; he did not round Cape Horn, but passed through the strait to which he gave his name, believing that it separated the southern tip of America from the great southern continent, *Terra Australis,* which was to haunt the twilight zone of the maps of the world and the minds of its explorers for more than a century. Magellan's ship reached the Spice Islands in the East Indies, and returned home by way of the Cape of Good Hope, completing the first circumnavigation of the globe. The keys of both these routes, it may be added, the Cape of Good Hope, and the Falkland Islands in the South Atlantic nearly five hundred miles from Cape Horn, came subsequently to be held by the British.

By Magellan's time Spain and Portugal were already competing for the empire of the world, and following a papal award—the first of the many partitions to which the Pacific was to be subject—the fixing of a dividing line between the two empires about 370 leagues west of the Cape Verde Islands was agreed to in the Treaty of Tordesillas, 1494. By 1515 Portugal had acquired a foothold in India and had captured Malacca on the Malay Peninsula; in 1529 a second partition awarded Portugal the control of the Spice Islands while leaving the Philippines in Spanish hands. The Portuguese empire in the southwest Pacific was, however, soon to disappear almost completely, after the first appearance of Dutch trading expeditions in 1595. The English East India Company was chartered in 1600, the Dutch East India Company in 1602. By 1605 the Dutch had inflicted defeats on the Portuguese and had established a protectorate over Amboyna; by 1609 they had assumed sovereignty over the Spice Islands, Batavia, in Java, being made the capital of Netherlands India in 1611. By 1641 the Portuguese had been ousted from the southwest Pacific save for their toehold in the eastern half of Timor, where the boundary between the Portuguese and Dutch sovereignty over a very primitive country and people was only agreed to—another partition—in 1859, and fixed by arbitration by the Hague Court in 1914.

The Dutch had, however, a more dogged rival than the Portuguese in the English of the time of James I. After the massacre of Amboyna in 1623, however, the British East India Company tacitly withdrew from the Indies and turned to the careless building of an empire in India, retaining, in this informal partition, only a few miserable factories on the outer coast of Sumatra. It was thus the Dutch who were to discover, though not to colonize, the great territories lying to the east and south of the Netherlands Indies.

William Janszoon explored the southwest coast of New Guinea and the Gulf of Carpenteria in Australia in 1605, though without realizing that the two were not a single landmass. In 1605, also, a Spanish expedition had sailed into the South Seas from South America; its commander, Quirós, discovered the New Hebrides, one of which he thought to be the *Terra Australis;* his second-in-command, Torres, discovered that New Guinea, where he died, was an island, and gave his name to the strait separating it from northern Australia. Knowledge of this discovery was, however, long lost, as was the discovery and naming of the Solomon Islands in 1567 by Mendaña, sailing from Peru; these were, indeed, the lost islands of the world for two centuries.

A series of Dutch voyages between 1616 and 1627 charted much of the west and part of the southern coasts of Australia, which was named New Holland. That these were parts of a single island was really proved by Tasman's epic voyages from Batavia in 1642 and 1644, in which Tasmania and New Zealand, the latter thought to be a projection of the murky southern continent, *Terra Australis,* were discovered. William Dampier, an Englishman on a semipiratical expedition in 1688, touched at western Australia, and by his account of his voyage revived interest in the region. In a later voyage in 1699, he established the insularity of New Britain, which he named (it had hitherto been thought to be part of New Guinea). Yet knowledge of the southwest Pacific remained so dim that in the early eighteenth century Swift could still quite plausibly locate Lilliput amid its waters.

The historic voyage of Captain Cook in the *Endeavour Bark* in 1769, a voyage of revolutionary consequence, was not, however, without immediate antecedents. Anson's voyage round the world, under the orders of the British Admiralty, between 1740 and 1744 (undertaken in connection with the War of Jenkins' Ear) had created new interest in the Pacific. Two captains of the Royal Navy, Wallis and Carteret, sailed for the Pacific in 1767. Wallis discovered and annexed Tahiti, which he named George the Third Island; Carteret, with a sick crew, discovered or rediscovered the Santa Cruz Islands and the Solomons, and showed that New Britain was really two islands, of which he named the second New Ireland. The visit of the great French soldier-navigator Bougainville to the Pacific in 1768, when he touched at Tahiti and made discoveries in Samoa, the New Hebrides, and the Louisiade Archipelago, brought to the scene another European power, one jealous both of empire and of its scientific prestige as the home of the *Encyclopédie*. Bougainville's voyage made doubly fateful the decision of the British Admiralty and the Royal Society to join hands in the expedition, to be commanded by Cook, to observe the transit of Venus between the earth and the sun in Tahiti (hence renamed the Society Islands) in 1769, and to continue westward to discover and to annex the old will-o'-the-wisp, the great southern continent, *Terra Australis*. This well-equipped expedition, well versed in previous discoveries, proved anew the existence of Torres Strait, proved the insularity of the two islands of New Zealand, came upon the southeast coast of Australia in 1770, botanized at Botany Bay and named the country New South Wales, and carried out "one of the most perilous feats of navigation ever accomplished," the tracing of the Great Barrier Reef. In his voyage in the *Resolution* in 1772–1774, Cook discovered and named New Caledonia, named the New Hebrides, named the Friendly Islands (Tonga) which Tasman had visited earlier, and by his prolonged exploration of Antarctica destroyed forever the legend of the great southern continent, "a feat of navigation such as no man before him had approached." His third voyage, in 1776, took him to the waters of the North Pacific, to Alaska and Bering Strait, and to the Sandwich Islands (Hawaii), the previous discovery of which by the Spaniards had long been forgotten, and where Cook himself met his death. By this time, and thanks very greatly to Cook, the map of the Pacific had been almost completely drawn, though almost all the lands of Oceania, and Australia itself, still remained virgin territory for annexation and colonization. It was not, however, until 1798 that Bass and Flinders confirmed that Tasmania was an island, separated from Australia by Bass Strait; and only Flinders' voyage round Australia in 1801-1803 finally dispatched the theory that a strait from the Gulf of Carpentaria southwards divided the continent, and proved that New Holland and New South Wales were parts of a single land. Nor was Australia crossed from south to north by land until 1861.[2]

Accounts of Captain Cook's voyages were something of a best seller, so that he was both a discoverer and a popularizer of the lands of the Pacific; the man of Tahiti became the noble savage *par excellence,* the unspoiled child of nature. Yet the first result of his discoveries seemed hardly auspicious—the decision of the British government to establish a convict settlement at Botany Bay to relieve the pressure of the convict population on the Thames-side hulks now that the American colonies could no longer be used as the destination for those sentenced to penal transportation. Nevertheless, the arrival of Captain Phillip and the "First Fleet" at Botany Bay in January, 1788, actually opened a new page in the history, not only of the Pacific, but also of the British Empire. For, without at first intending it, Great Britain came to establish not one but five colonies in Australia, preëmpting the whole continent to enlarge the empire which the American Revolution had previously diminished. The visit of the French exploring vessels to Australian waters, the *Géographe* in 1802, and the *Astrolabe* in 1824, led to the occupations respectively of Tasmania and Port Phillip (Melbourne)

---

[2] James A. Williamson, *Short History of British Expansion* (2d ed.; New York, 1931), Vol. I, *passim; Cambridge History of the British Empire,* Vol. VII (1933), pp. 24–53; *ibid.,* Vol. I (1929), pp. 535–537; Ernest Scott, *Short History of Australia* (2d ed.; London, 1918).

and of Swan River in Western Australia; but it was free emigration from the teeming, expansionist Britain of Victoria's reign, supported at first by some direct government backing, that really planted the Australian colonies firmly in the soil, and rapidly made up for the continent's centuries of isolation from the rest of the world. As free settlers came to exceed the convict population, the demand for self-government, that inalienable birthright of the British subject everywhere, became unanswerable, and progressively the five mainland colonies and Tasmania gained representative assemblies and responsible cabinets. The curse of transportation was lifted from New South Wales in 1840 and from Tasmania in 1853; in Western Australia it lasted, by local request, until 1867.

At first these tiny colonies, separated from one another and from the outside world by vast distances, had but a slight influence upon the destinies of the southwest Pacific. By degrees they grew, until their wool, their grain, their dairy products, and the gold of Ballarat and Bendigo and Kalgoorlie, gave them a major place in the markets of the world. Their people, coming mainly from the better sections of the British working class at a time when trade unionism was making rapid strides, demanded advanced conditions of work and a fair measure of practical socialism in their new land, and Australia came to have one of the highest standards of living in the world, an elaborate system of labor arbitration and conciliation courts, and a good deal of advanced social legislation. In time the colonies assumed responsibility for their land defenses. By 1900 they were ready to federate, and to establish the Commonwealth of Australia. But, though the Australians now spoke with one voice, as a Dominion, that voice was still weak, partly because they were still few in numbers, partly because, apart from a small squadron of their own, they must depend on the British navy for their defense by sea. Thus, though the Commonwealth gave a certain solidity to the concerns of the Pacific by spreading civilization, if rather thinly, over a large land area, yet it continued, down to 1914, to suffer from the handicap under which the colonies had labored previously, that they could bring pressure on the British government in its policies in the Pacific but could not determine them. To the world at large they had no official voice but that of Britain; and Britannia, though she had perforce to heed the tiresome cries which came from these children of her own in the Pacific, customarily decided on her policies in the Pacific by reference to concerns exclusively British and European, thousands of miles away. Even the medium of communications was faulty, for the colonies could only intercede with the Colonial Office, and it in turn might intercede, and that but feebly, with the Foreign Office, when some matter of Australian and international concern was pending. The war of 1914–1918 began to teach the world that a Dominion was, in most regards, a sovereign state; the Paris peace conference and the League of Nations recognized this; and Australia's vigor and assertiveness and industrial strength have underscored it. Today Australia no longer speaks through Great Britain, and in Pacific affairs her voice is now listened to with respect; but, as we shall see, it was not always so.[3]

New Zealand, far smaller than Australia in size and population, and totally different in climate and vegetation and terrain, nevertheless has this in common with its larger neighbor, that it too has been a stabilizing influence in the Pacific, with a self-reliant British population, and a place in the world's markets (though mainly in Britain's markets) for its chilled lamb and its butter, but has at the same time been able only to protest or to influence, never to dictate, Britain's policies in the Pacific which might affect it closely. Its colonization, too, was originally unintended. It was the presence of British missionaries, whalers, and traders, and their conflicts with the warlike Maoris, plus once more the fear of French colonial ventures, that led the British government to annex the islands in 1840 and to make the peculiar Treaty of Waitangi with the Maoris, whereby, in return for ceding New Zealand, they were guaranteed all their vast tribal lands save those which the government might

[3] See, in general, Scott, *A Short History of Australia,* and C. Hartley Grattan, *Introducing Australia* (New York, 1942).

then or subsequently purchase by negotiation from them. The British settlers progressively achieved self-government, and used it to form for themselves what is perhaps the most advanced body of social legislation enjoyed by any country in the world. In 1907 New Zealand was given the title of Dominion. Yet its spirit, though of the highest gallantry, as two wars have nobly shown, has been less independent of Britain than Australia's, and its influence on British and on Pacific policies has been, though important, far from decisive.[4]

Before the Australian colonies were many years old, Britain was developing her interests farther to the northwest in the Pacific. The fortunes of the war against Revolutionary and Napoleonic France made Britain an adversary of the Dutch. This provided the opportunity for an attack upon the Netherlands Indies, which was strongly urged by an ambitious and clearheaded East India Company official, Stamford Raffles, who at the time was Assistant Secretary of the newly created province of Penang, established by the company in 1804. Penang had been ceded, for an annual rent, under agreement made with the Rajah of Kedah in Malay in 1786; the mainland strip, Province Wellesley, was added in 1800 to provide for the suppression of piracy and to serve as a source for ship's timber which the war was making a precious commodity. The British expedition against Java was quickly successful, and Raffles, as Lieutenant Governor of Java from 1811 until its return to the Dutch after 1815, gave it an enlightened administration. Disconsolate over the reëstablishment of Dutch power, Raffles sought for another base in the area, from which Britain's naval and commercial strength in the East Indies could be protected. He found it in Singapore Island, which, with the support of the Governor General of India, Lord Hastings, he acquired for the East India Company in 1819 by treaty with the Sultan of Johore. This led to disputes with the Dutch, followed by intermittent negotiations in London from 1820 to 1824. In the latter year, by the Treaty of Lon-

[4] W. P. Morrell, *New Zealand* (London, 1935); W. Pember Reeves, *New Zealand* (3d ed.; Boston, 1925), originally published as *The Long White Cloud*.

don, an important partition of interests was made. Britain ceded to the Dutch Bencoolen and all its rights in Sumatra, thus recognizing Dutch omnipotence in the Netherlands Indies; the Dutch ceded to Great Britain Malacca and the Dutch establishments in India, recognized the British possession of Singapore, and agreed to a settlement of their debts to Great Britain.[5]

Thus were the Straits Settlements (Singapore, Malacca, Penang, and Province Wellesley) established; they remained under the Indian government until 1867, when they became a separate crown colony. The association with them of the Federated Malay States of Perak, Selangor, Negri Sembilan, and Pahang developed between 1874 and 1895 as a result of the inevitable border troubles between colonial and native territories, and the economic development of the southern and western parts of the Malay Peninsula. In the Federated States the power of the native authorities became as much a fiction as the federation itself; it was essentially an area under crown colony government, closely associated with the Straits Settlements. The Unfederated Malay States of Johore, Kedah, Kelantan, Trengganu, and Perlis are, with the exception of the first two, largely undeveloped; native government remained relatively untrammeled, save for the presence of a British advisor and the surrender of independence in foreign affairs. Kedah, Kelantan, Trengganu, and Perlis were states of Siam until 1909, when Siam ceded suzerain rights over them to Britain. This partition of interests was the result of frontier troubles and the desire of Siam to be relieved of certain British extraterritorial rights and power of interference in Siamese affairs conceded in 1855, which was made a *quid pro quo* for the transfer of suzerainty over the border states. It was not until the twentieth century that tin and rubber made the British stake in Malaya of outstanding importance.[6]

---
[5] *Cambridge History of the British Empire*, Vol. II (1940), pp. 592–614.
[6] *Dominions Office and Colonial Office List, 1937*, pp. 364–397; *Encyclopaedia Britannica;* W. E. Simnett, *The British Colonial Empire* (London, 1942), pp. 119–125; Lennox A. Mills, *Brittish Rule in Eastern Asia* (Minneapolis, 1942); Virginia Thompson, *Postmortem on Malaya* (New York, 1943).

Britain's other interests in the East Indies developed in the same way. Brunei, a native state which is little more than a ghost of the Sultanate which once included most of Borneo, has been under British protection by treaty since 1888, though there had been various British trading settlements in the area in earlier times. These gave rise, through cessions of 1877 and 1878, to British North Borneo, which since 1882 has been governed by a British chartered company, the British North Borneo Company, under British protection. This form of government, unique in later years amid the chameleon-like diversity which is the British Empire, had, of course, earlier been shared by Rhodesia, Nigeria, and Uganda, and earlier still by Pennsylvania, Maryland, and even Massachusetts and Virginia. Near by, in Sarawak, Sir James Brooke, the "white rajah," had ruled since 1842. A soldier serving the East India Company, he inherited considerable property and in 1838 fitted out an expedition of his own with the avowed object of rescuing the islands of the Indian archipelago from barbarism and ridding the seas of piracy. His services in the wars of one of the rajahs won him his principality and the title, Rajah of Sarawak, given him by the Sultan of Brunei. Britain recognized this as an independent state in 1864, and took it under its protection by agreement in 1888. Sir James's successor is still the "white rajah," though at present without a home.[7]

We have still to account for the partitioning of the vast stretches of Oceania. This melodrama, the action of which takes place mainly before 1899, has for its principal actors the great powers, Britain, France, the United States, and, in the later scenes, Germany; Australia and New Zealand are cast, sometimes unwillingly, in supporting roles; while the helpless native peoples of the area are merely the picturesque 'supers.' Principal elements in the play of rival forces are the following: the omnipresence of the British navy, which in 1869 had commands at the Pacific station, the China

---

[7] *Dominions Office and Colonial Office List, 1937*, pp. 516–522; Simnett, pp. 125–128.

station, the East India station, and the Australia station, and in 1913 had squadrons of the "Eastern Fleet" stationed at China, Australia, the East Indies, the Cape of Good Hope, and the west coast of America, these commands still surviving in rather different form in 1939;[8] the use of British and other warships for the policing of turbulent island populations; the 'warship diplomacy' practiced especially by the Germans and the French; the activities of the missionaries, and their rivalries, especially that between the Roman Catholic missions and the Protestant, leading, through the recognition of native kingdoms which were really only missionary kingdoms, to the establishment of a 'protectorate,' or outright annexation; the activities of the whalers, and later of the traders and planters concerned with copra or sandalwood or guano; the labor needs of plantations, leading to the unsavory practice of "blackbirding," and the intervention which this necessitated; the quest for coaling stations of navies and merchant vessels; the quest for islets suitable for landing stations for a submarine cable across the Pacific, and the corresponding interest in our day in islands to serve as stepping-stones and weather-forecasting stations for transpacific airplane services; and finally, the great international rivalries determined in part by ambitions in Europe and Africa rather than in the Pacific. The international discords which these forces produced were for the most part settled peaceably, and mainly by a series of partitions, made easier by the chronic reluctance of the British government, and especially of the Colonial Office, to take on new commitments in the Pacific by the annexation of territory for Great Britain.[9]

Down to about 1850 only the British and French, and to a less degree the Americans, were involved in rivalry over Oceania. Despite the discoveries and annexations of Cook and his contempo-

---
[8] *Whitaker's Almanack*, 1869, p. 144; 1913, p. 237; 1939, p. 418.
[9] See, besides the more specific references given later, Scholefield, *The Pacific, Its Past and Future;* Jean I. Brooks, *International Rivalry in the Pacific Islands, 1800-1875* (Berkeley, 1941); Beatrice Orent and Pauline Reinsch, "Sovereignty over Islands in the Pacific," *American Journal of International Law*, Vol. XXXV (July, 1941), pp. 443-461; K. L. P. Martin, *Missionaries and Annexation in the Pacific* (Oxford, 1924).

raries, the British government refused to extend its sovereignty over any of the islands, and it was left for the missionaries to bring them into international prominence. The sailing of the *Duff,* chartered by the London Missionary Society, was therefore epochal; after its arrival in Tahiti, missions were established there and in the Tonga Islands and the Marquesas in 1797. Tahiti became a center of British influence and civilization, and under the guidance of the great consul-missionary Pritchard the native government of Queen Pomare was that of the model missionary kingdom. Queen Pomare's petition for British protection in 1825, following the visit of French and Russian ships, was, however, refused, and the arrival of two French Roman Catholic priests in 1836, harbingers of the Vicar-Apostolic of Oceania, promised only trouble.

The French, under Louis Philippe, were looking to an active colonial policy to revive the glories of the *patrie,* and were not prepared to tolerate the reverses which their priests met at the hands of the Protestant Queen Pomare. The French frigate *Venus,* under the command of the most vigorous of France's 'warship diplomats,' Dupetit-Thouars, compelled the Queen to make a treaty with France and pay an indemnity for past misdeeds, in 1838. Queen Victoria refused the protection which her dusky sister ruler in the Pacific then sought for, and Captain La Place of the French frigate *L'Artémise,* and later Dupetit-Thouars in 1842, were able to obtain further concessions from Queen Pomare, leading to the establishment of a French protectorate. British influence was restored by the arrival of H.M.S. *Talbot* with the timely gift from Queen to Queen of a carriage and a set of drawing-room furniture in 1843, but Dupetit-Thouars soon regained the upper hand, arresting Consul Pritchard and hauling down and trampling on the Queen's flag, which included the British crown in its design, saying, "Here goes the crown of England once more in the dirt!" Thus did the French annex Tahiti, and oust the British from the islands. This was recognized by the British government in a declaration signed with the French in London in 1847, which provided that some of the outer islands should remain a French protectorate, under Queen Pomare's rule; and this arrangement, galling to the French, endured till after the Queen's death, when French annexation of the remaining islands took place, to be finally recognized by Britain in the Anglo-French convention of 1887.[10]

Meanwhile, in Hawaii (the Sandwich Islands) the tragic visit of Cook was followed by two visits by Vancouver in 1792 and 1794. The British flag was hoisted, but George III's government refused to ratify this action. British and Russian whalers frequently visited the islands in the ensuing years, but the first settlement of Occidentals was left to the American Board of Missions, which, influenced by the presence at American universities of Hawaiian youths brought by whalers and trading ships, decided in 1820 to send missionaries to the islands at a time when the United States had as yet scarcely a foothold on the Pacific Coast. The London Missionary Society, whose deputation arrived in 1822, therefore decided to leave this mission field to the Americans; similarly, George IV, though he feted the Hawaiian king and queen in England on their visit in 1824, during which they unfortunately died of measles, would not agree to the annexation of the islands. An American consulate was established in 1822, and a treaty of friendship with the United States was made in 1826. The presence of French Roman Catholic missionaries after 1826, however, disturbed the peace of the islands, and in the 1830's the ubiquitous Dupetit-Thouars arrived with his persuasive warship. American influence, based on a considerable number of American residents, came, however, to predominate, and, imperialism being still frowned on in the young Republic, this meant the strengthening of Hawaii as an independent kingdom. Following a brief interlude in 1843 when Captain Lord George Paulet of H.M.S. *Carysfort* so terrorized King Kamehameha III that he ceded his kingdom to the noble captain personally, Britain and France issued a joint declaration recognizing Hawaii as an independent state, which, under increasing American influ-

---

[10] Scholefield, *op. cit.*, pp. 5-31.

ence, strengthened as America's interest in the Pacific grew, it continued to be.[11]

Samoa, though visited by various British and French scientific expeditions between 1768 and 1838, did not receive the message of the gospel until 1828, and then only from native converts from Tonga; a small British community of traders, planters, and whalers subsequently grew up on the beaches. In 1839 the islands received a very significant visit from what was the first American scientific expedition in the Pacific, authorized by Act of Congress in 1836 as a result of the interest stirred up by the voyages of American whalers in Pacific waters. Captain Charles Wilkes of the *Vincennes*, on this epic voyage, established in Samoa an American consul in the person of John C. Williams, son of the eminent British missionary of the London Missionary Society, John Williams, who was active there.[12] Wilkes also visited Fiji, where he established an American vice-consul; the Fiji Islands had been the resort of whalers, traders, and settlers from Australia since the first arrival of Wesleyan missionaries in 1835. In the Tongas, Wesleyan missionaries were active after 1826, though handicapped by French Roman Catholic priests, supported by a French frigate, some ten years later. Here, as in Samoa, the natives developed a terribly time-consuming passion for cricket. The only other islands at all affected by 'civilization' in that period were New Caledonia and the New Hebrides. The former was visited by French missionaries, who claimed the country for France, in 1843; but under British protests the claim was renounced. However, in 1851 a landing party from a French man-of-war took possession, and French annexation was declared in 1853. In the New Hebrides, missionaries of the London Missionary Society arrived in 1839, and in the succeeding years this barren field was bravely worked by Presbyterian missions from Scotland, Canada, Australia, and New Zealand, from among which the savage

[11] Scholefield, *op. cit.*, pp. 32-42.
[12] Scholefield, *op. cit.*, p. 148; George H. Ryden, *Foreign Policy of the United States in Relation to Samoa* (New Haven, 1933), pp. 5-24; Sylvia Masterman, *Origins of International Rivalry in Samoa, 1845-1884* (Stanford Univ. Press, 1934).

natives made many martyrs. Here, as elsewhere, the British government refused to heed demands for annexation; nor would it listen to the scheme of a Pacific Federation proposed in 1847 by Sir George Grey, Governor of New Zealand—the first instance of a suggestion of policy made by the infant British colonies of the Pacific.[13]

After the middle of the century the pace of international rivalries in the Pacific quickened. Four new factors had to be reckoned with: the development of German interests, eventually supported by Bismarck and the government of the German Empire; the growing concern of the United States in the affairs of the Pacific; the problem of "blackbirding," the recruitment of native laborers (Kanakas) by Europeans by kidnapping, violence, or deceit; and the claim of Australia and New Zealand to be heard when Pacific matters were under discussion.

The first scene of the new clash of interests was Samoa. It was here that the powerful Hamburg shipping and trading company of Godeffroy and Son, "far-seeing, industrious, and unscrupulous," first established its connections in the Pacific in the 1850's. In the next twenty years it and other German concerns established posts all over the South Seas, in the Fiji, Gilbert, Ellice, Tonga, Marshall, and Solomon Islands, New Britain, the New Hebrides, and the Carolines. Gradually the Germans obtained almost all the copra trade of the Pacific. In Samoa, by virtue of their superior numbers, their settlers came to predominate over those of Great Britain and the United States. The isle of Apia became the most important center of German influence in the Pacific, and was the headquarters of an energetic consul. In the 1870's German warships were constantly stationed in the Pacific, and the government decided to obtain a coaling station in Samoa. Godeffroy and Son went bankrupt, but were replaced by a new company, the Deutsche See Handels Gesellschaft, whose capital seemed far larger than its immediate activities warranted. Again New Zealand, this time in the person of Julius

---

[13] Scholefield, *op. cit.*, pp. 73–74, 197–199, 244 ff., 274–280.

Vogel, then Agent General, urged the making of a British federation of all the islands while there was yet time; but, as before, the plea fell on deaf ears.

The United States was also bestirring itself in the Pacific, and beginning to realize its strategic interest in the area. The Navy was concerned over the protection of American trade routes to the Orient, and saw the need of bases in the North Pacific, as at Hawaii, and in the South Pacific, as at Samoa. Californians were developing an interest in Samoan real estate. William H. Webb was pushing his plans for an American steamship line to New Zealand, and urged the need of American coaling stations along the route. These various pressures explain the American annexation of Midway Island (discovered by an American shipmaster in 1859) by Captain Reynolds, U.S.S. *Lackawanna,* on orders of the Navy Department in 1867, and the Act of Congress of 1869, never carried out, for the deepening of the harbor there. They explain, too, the agreement negotiated in Samoa in 1872 by Commander Meade, of the U.S.S. *Narragansett,* authorizing the establishment of a United States naval station at Pago Pago. This agreement was not ratified by the Senate, but President Grant sent Colonel Steinberger to Samoa as United States special commissioner. Steinberger's intrigues, which made him for a time virtual premier of Samoa, and involved him in some shady dealings with Godeffroy and Son, eventually led to his deportation, not without the help of the local American consul.

Increasing German pressure in Samoa, including the making of a treaty with the natives in 1877, led, after the visit of the chief, La Mamea, to Washington in that year, to the decision of the United States to break its long-held tradition of avoiding entangling alliances by making a treaty with Samoa in 1878. The United States could have had Samoa for the asking, as far as the Samoan chiefs were concerned; instead, the treaty was made, giving Americans freedom of entry and trade, transferring Pago Pago by deed to the United States, and promising that if Samoa should become involved in difficulties with other powers the United States would use its good offices on its behalf. The Germans at once claimed that this violated their treaty of 1877, and obtained a new one giving them special privileges and the right also to establish a naval and coaling station. The British, by a treaty also negotiated in 1879, obtained similar rights. Thus the three powers were encamped in these small islands, presided over by a native government so weak that it was little more than a football for the rival foreign groups. Twenty years of disorder in Samoa were to follow.[14]

British policy, here passive enough, was meanwhile somewhat more active in the Fiji Islands, where "blackbirding," particularly for the Queensland cotton and sugar plantations, stirred up native hostility which led to punitive expeditions by British warships and protests from the French in New Caledonia. The very able British consul in Fiji, J. B. Thurston, did his best to check the evil, but after the murder of Bishop Patteson at Nukapu in 1871, more definite action became necessary and Parliament passed, in 1872, the Pacific Islanders Protection Act, setting up a licensing system for recruiters of native labor and giving colonial courts jurisdiction over infringements of the act. Real regulation was, however, impossible as long as a congeries of cosmopolitan beachcombers occupied shores where no adequate native or European authority existed. Britain, which had turned down the several offers of the native chiefs, under the influence of the all-powerful consul, W. T. Pritchard, son of the Tahiti missionary, to transfer the islands to Queen Victoria in 1857–1859, and had rejected further proposals of annexation in 1870, strongly urged by a conference of the Australian colonies at Melbourne, finally and reluctantly decided, on Thurston's advice, to annex the Fiji Islands in 1874. Following this, in 1875, the office of British High Commissioner for the western Pacific, always held concurrently with the governorship of Fiji, was created to regulate labor recruiting. The High Commissioner, more particularly under the Order in Council of 1877, has jurisdiction over British subjects

---

[14] Ryden, *op. cit.*, pp. xi–xviii (introduction by John Bassett Moore) and *passim*; Masterman, *op. cit., passim*; Orent and Reinsch, *American Journal of International Law*, Vol. XXXV, pp. 443 ff.; Scholefield, *op. cit.*, pp. 97–101, 148–152.

in all islands in the western Pacific outside of the British colonies, with power to bring them to trial and deportation; his writ extended to the Tonga, Samoa, Ellice, Gilbert, Marshall, Caroline, Solomon, and Santa Cruz islands, New Guinea, New Britain, New Ireland, and the Louisiades, and all other islands in the western Pacific Ocean not within the jurisdiction of any civilized power.[15]

These activities of the British spurred on, if spur was needed, the expansive spirit of Germany in the Pacific. In 1882 the Kolonialverein was founded, and began to paint the possibilities of German enterprise in the Pacific in glowing colors. Bismarck now decided that Germany must build an overseas empire, not so much to gain the place in the sun which, as a great power, it was entitled to, as to provoke a quarrel with the British Empire and so to further a German entente with France.[16] He therefore supported the work of diplomatic agents masquerading as itinerant scientists, like Dr. Karl Peters and Dr. Nachtigal, and the efforts of German traders and missionaries, with the inevitable warships, and rapidly added South West Africa, Tanganyika, Togoland, and the Cameroons to the German Empire.[17] In the Pacific, much could be built on the foundations laid by Godeffroy and Son, and, apart from Germany's large interests in Samoa, New Guinea seemed to offer a fruitful field for colonization.

The large island of New Guinea, so vital to Australia's defense, had been proclaimed to be under British sovereignty by two East Indiamen in 1792, though this had never been accepted by the British government. The Dutch from the Netherlands Indies established their title to the western part of the island in 1828 by occupation and an arrangement with the Sultan of Tidore. In 1842 the British Admiralty ordered a survey to be made of Torres Strait, and in 1846 Captain Yule of H.M.S. *Bramble* hoisted the British

---

[15] Scholefield, *op. cit.*, pp. 50–72, 74–96.
[16] A. J. P. Taylor, *Germany's First Bid for Colonies, 1884–1885* (New York, 1938), reviewed by Mary E. Townsend in the *American Historical Review*, Vol. XLIV (July, 1939), pp. 899–901.
[17] See, for instance, Halford L. Hoskins, *European Imperialism in Africa* (New York, 1930).

flag at Cape Possession. This action was ignored, and colonization companies formed in New South Wales in the 1860's were actively discouraged by the Colonial Office. New South Wales continued to urge annexation of New Guinea and various other islands of the western Pacific, and in 1874 the Colonial Secretary, Lord Carnarvon, asked the Australian colonies if they would contribute to the resultant expenses. New South Wales and New Zealand agreed, but Queensland did not, and annexation was therefore again refused.

German activities in the Pacific, and rumors that Germany intended to occupy New Guinea, revived Australian agitation in 1882, and, after a cabled offer of Queensland's to annex it and bear the cost had been refused by the Colonial Office, Queensland went ahead and annexed New Guinea in the name of Queen Victoria in 1883; this ceremony was performed at Port Moresby by a police magistrate. Victoria, New South Wales, and South Australia cabled their approval to London. Gladstone's government was, however, from a healthy reaction to Disraeli's flambcyant and costly imperialism, in no mood for such adventures; moreover, the Foreign Secretary informed the Colonial Secretary (such was and is the interoffice routine of Whitehall) that Germany had no intentions toward this territory. Queensland's act of annexation was therefore repudiated. This led to an intercolonial convention at Sydney at which Britain's action was severely condemned and an offer to share the expenses of annexation made; this convention, though it had no immediate results, did, along with the colonies' realization of their impotence regarding British policy in the Pacific, help to bring about the Australian federation.

German activity was naturally stimulated still further by this exhibition of imperial apathy and Australian interest. Negotiations were begun, quite unknown to the Australians, who were not consulted, between Great Britain and Germany to prevent a clash of interests between their subjects in the area. The British government stated its intention to declare a protectorate over the part of New Guinea of concern to Australia (the southeast part); Germany expressed interest in the northern part. What hampered negotiations was that the Colonial Office and the Foreign Office were at cross purposes over annexation, the latter opposing action for fear of annoying Germany, whose good will Britain needed to support her position on the Egyptian international commission of European bondholders (the Caisse de la Dette) against France—another place where Disraeli's imperialism was being overtaken by its nemesis.[18]

The two powers agreed to appoint a joint commission, which should meet at Fiji to negotiate the matter of territorial spheres of influence in the Pacific and settle disputed claims in Samoa; and Britain went ahead with her expressed intention, and proclaimed a protectorate over southeastern New Guinea in October and November, 1884. Thereupon Germany, whose agent, Dr. Finsch, had been actively engaged in a "scientific mission" on the north coast of New Guinea, raised the German flag and annexed northeastern New Guinea and New Britain in December, 1884. The howls of rage which greeted the news in Australia are understandable enough; but the indignation expressed in England is not, since now it merely seems to have been a case of one plunderer of native territory getting the jump on another. The negotiations in Berlin had been ambiguous, but the British apparently expected the questions at issue to be decided by the joint commission at Fiji. Hence the protests against the German coup before that commission had met.

Great Britain was not, however, in a position to bruise too easily over the matter. There was trouble enough in Samoa and Tonga, in Egypt and the Sudan, and in East Africa; and Germany, moreover, shrewdly made an agreement with France in 1885, renouncing all claims to Tahiti and the New Hebrides, where the French were now active, in return for the right to recruit native labor there. Germany was also pushing its power in the Pacific by challenging the reality of Spain's authority over the Caroline and Marshall Islands, which were vaguely associated with Spanish power in the Philip-

[18] R. C. K. Ensor, *England, 1870–1914* (Oxford, 1936), pp. 77–85.

pines. This led to a race between German and Spanish warships to raise flags over the Caroline Islands, the Germans raising theirs at Yap in 1885 under the very eyes of a Spanish commander. Feeling ran high in Spain, and the King insisted that the matter be submitted to the arbitration of the Pope, to which Bismarck agreed. The Pope's award gave the islands to Spain, subject to Germany's having equal trading rights. The two powers agreed to this, and Germany's penetration of the islands was thereafter rapid.

In these circumstances, the British were glad to negotiate the Anglo-German Declaration signed at Berlin in 1886. This important partition defined British and German spheres in the Pacific, each party renouncing all intentions to annex or interfere within the sphere of the other. Germany's sphere included northeastern New Guinea, New Britain, and the islands north of the equator from 165° W. Long. to 130° E. Long.[19] It is interesting to note that in this same year Germany and Britain, with France, agreed to the delimitation by an impartial commission of their claims in East Africa and on the coast north and south of Zanzibar.

It remained for the British to provide for that part of New Guinea which they had salvaged from Germany. With the Dutch, a boundary line dividing the British and Dutch territories was fixed by a convention signed at The Hague in 1895. At the Colonial Conference held in 1887 in London in connection with the Golden Jubilee, Queensland, New South Wales, and Victoria agreed to guarantee £10,000 per year for ten years toward the administration of British New Guinea if sovereignty should be proclaimed in place of the protectorate. This was done in 1888, when Sir William MacGregor began his successful term as Administrator. In 1898, Joseph Chamberlain urged the Australian colonies, since they were close at hand, to take over full responsibility for British New Guinea. The negotiations for federation delayed the matter, but after the Commonwealth had come into existence Britain transferred New Guinea to it, Australian acceptance being provided for by the Papua Act

[19] Scholefield, *op. cit.*, pp. 102–143, 179–183.

1905, of the Commonwealth parliament. The Papua Act, which anticipated some of the later ideas about mandates, provided for a modified form of crown colony government, though land was available to white settlers only on lease, rather than ownership, and the idea of trusteeship in the interest of the natives was insisted on. Under Sir Hubert Murray, MacGregor's successor as Lieutenant Governor, the Australian administration of the territory of Papua was, as it remains, enlightened and successful, to the surprise of those who argued Australia's incapacity for conducting a colonial government in the light of its poor record with its own aborigines.[20]

Meanwhile, affairs in the unhappy islands of Samoa had passed through various crises. Germans, British, and Americans intrigued with the various native factions and against each other. New Zealand urged Britain to annex Samoa and Tonga and offered to bear the cost; the threat of its government to go ahead and do this on its own initiative nearly brought the Colonial Secretary in London to a state of apoplexy. Some of the Samoan chiefs sent a petition to Great Britain asking for annexation. Hearing of this, German agents on the spot secured, with the help of two warships, a treaty from the natives giving Germany virtually sovereign powers over Samoa (November, 1884), and shortly afterward raised the German flag over two of the islands. Though Anglo-German relations were strained by this development, a rupture was avoided by the appointment of the joint commission resulting primarily from the New Guinea crisis. The commissioners, however, J. B. Thurston and Dr. Krauel, could reach no agreement, and anarchy increased in Samoa, where the German flag had been lowered, partly owing to the persuasion of British and American naval captains, and where the king, Malietoa, was challenged by insurgent groups.

Then Bismarck, taking advantage of a report of drunken insults flung at German citizens by Samoans, declared war on Malietoa—

[20] Scholefield, *op. cit.,* pp. 144–147; *Cambridge History of the British Empire,* Vol. VII, pp. 360, 515–516, 622–624; Sir Hubert Murray, *Papua or British New Guinea* (London, 1912), and *Papua of Today; or an Australian Colony in the Making* (London, 1925).

a case of the eagle declaring war on the sparrow. On the advice of the British and American consuls, Malietoa fled into the bush, so that the 'war' proved to be bloodless, and a new native government under King Tamasese was set up. This was really a German government backed up by warships, but even so it faced a serious rebellion by Malietoa's forces, and German support of Tamasese's government with warships was somewhat hampered by the action of American warships in shadowing the German. In one engagement seventeen Germans were killed and thirty-nine wounded when supporting Tamasese's forces against the rebels. German reprisals against native villages followed. In Washington the United States government, using its good offices under the treaty of 1878, called a conference with British and German representatives in 1887, but this broke down in the sweltering heat of a Washington summer. The great powers might have come to blows in Samoa but for the hurricane of Apia, so vividly described by Robert Louis Stevenson,[21] which destroyed most of the German and American armadas. A more conciliatory spirit followed; Bismarck rebuked the German consul for some of his actions, Malietoa was restored as king, and the three powers met in the Berlin Conference of 1889. Here the United States again accepted an entangling alliance by agreeing to a sort of 'condominium' for Samoa. The independence of Samoa as a native kingdom was recognized, but there was to be a supreme court with a European judge, and at Apia a municipal council, under a neutral chairman, representing the three powers. A year later, Britain ended other colonial disputes with Germany by the agreement which gave Britain exclusive rights in Uganda, Zanzibar, and Nyasaland in return for the cession of Heligoland and certain territories in South West Africa and the Cameroons to Germany.

A feeble native government overlooked by three foreign powers inevitably meant only continuing disorder in Samoa. By 1899 the situation became intolerable, when native factions fought over

---

[21] See his *Footnote to History* and *Vailima Letters* for this period of Samoa's history.

the succession to the throne following Malietoa's death. A three-power commission was unable to reach any agreement. Germany then urged the United States to press Britain to agree to the triple partition of Samoa among the three powers. Britain's "splendid isolation" was never less splendid and more lonely than in that year, when the Boer War was imminent; and Lord Salisbury was glad to liquidate any unfinished diplomatic business in Samoa and elsewhere. The result was an Anglo-German treaty preceding a tripartite convention signed at Berlin by British, American, and German representatives (1899). By the first Britain gave up all her rights in Samoa, and Germany in return gave up her rights in Tonga, agreed to shifts in the demarcation line in the Solomons, and made certain concessions in West Africa and elsewhere. By the tripartite convention Samoa was partitioned between Germany and the United States, the latter obtaining sovereignty over Tutuila (including Pago Pago).[22]

These arrangements of 1899 made possible the final disposition of various other islands. New Zealand, furious over the surrender, behind her back, of British rights in Samoa which she, at least, valued highly, was appeased by the British annexation of the Cook Islands, which were transferred to New Zealand by an order in council in 1901. A British protectorate was established over the Tonga Islands (1900). The Gilbert and Ellice Islands, lying within the British sphere under the 1886 agreement with Germany, were made British protectorates in 1896 and 1897; Ocean Island was annexed in 1900; and the whole area was made a crown colony, governed from Ocean Island, in 1915. A protectorate over the British share of the Solomon Islands (including Guadalcanal and Tulagi) was proclaimed in 1893, and was later extended to include the Santa Cruz and certain other islands.[23]

One further important area of conflict in the southwest Pacific still remained, involving Great Britain and France, bitter colonial

[22] Scholefield, *op. cit.*, pp. 152–178; Ryden, *op. cit.*, pp. xi–xviii and *passim*.
[23] Scholefield, *op. cit.*, pp. 198–215, 272–273.

rivals in Africa and elsewhere at the end of the nineteenth century. This was the New Hebrides, the position of which made them of interest to Australia also. Though for many years the only missionaries to brave the savage country were British, the French missionaries from the Loyalty Islands (a French protectorate, near New Caledonia, since 1845) eventually intruded themselves into the New Hebrides and threatened to oust the British. The Australians were up in arms at this, but Britain was adamant against annexation, and the only result of Australian clamor was a French protest, which led to an Anglo-French understanding of 1878 by which each power disavowed intentions against the islands' independence. French colonizing activities increased, however, leading to more Australian petitions, and a new understanding in 1883. The Australians were also incensed at this time by the freedom given to certain French convicts from the penal colony in New Caledonia to leave the island, provided they did not return to France, and by the expressed intention of the French to increase the number of prisoners sent to New Caledonia (the *récidivistes*). Too many French convicts were in the habit of turning up at Australian ports. At the intercolonial convention at Sydney in 1883 the New Hebrides were almost as much discussed as New Guinea. Germany's success then only made the matter of the New Hebrides seem more urgent.

Yet nothing was done till 1886, when the French established two military posts on the New Hebrides. This action resulted in a British protest, followed by negotiations which culminated in the Anglo-French Convention of 1887. This, unlike most settlements in Pacific diplomacy, did not partition the islands, but left them independent, the lives and property of Europeans to be protected by a joint naval commission of British and French officers. This 'condominium' has never resulted in anything but pandemonium in the New Hebrides. Yet because the French would not give up their rights, and the British, under Australian and New Zealand pressure, could not, it has remained until today, being strengthened by a convention in 1906, following the cementing of the Entente Cordiale which ended so many colonial disputes between Britain and France. The British and French each maintain small government staffs to care for their own nationals; the joint naval commission still exists, partly to settle disputes between the natives; and on top of all this there is a Joint Court made up of a British judge and a French judge, presided over by a neutral president to be appointed by the King of Spain. The president was for many years the Count de Buena Esperanza, deaf, knowing little English or French and none of the native tongues, yet performing his simple duties for a very handsome salary. Thus pandemonium, European-born, reigns in the "savage civilization" of the cannibals.[24]

As the political map of the southwest Pacific was thus assuming, by the end of the nineteenth century, its modern form, the Spanish-American War over Cuba in 1898 came to bring further readjustments. The United States acquired the Philippines, Guam, and Wake Island from Spain, and in the same year assumed sovereignty over the Hawaiian Islands, whose nominally independent and unstable government had long been dominated by the large American colony in the islands. Thus did the United States take her place as one of the major powers in the Pacific, a position strengthened before 1914 by the expansion of the American navy and the opening of the Panama Canal. Germany, following Spain's defeat, bargained with her to obtain her remaining possessions in the Pacific, which lay within the German sphere under the Anglo-German treaty of 1886. The Caroline, Pelew, and Marianne Islands, excepting Guam, were thus bought by Germany from Spain in 1899.[25]

Guano and cables determined the sovereignty of the few remaining reefs and atolls unappropriated by the forces of civilization. Certain islands, discovered by American whalers, were temporarily occupied in the 1870's and 1880's by Americans interested in the

[24] Scholefield, *op. cit.*, pp. 246–272; Tom Harrisson, *Savage Civilization* (New York, 1937).
[25] Scholefield, *op. cit.*, pp. 42–49, 183–186.

guano deposits, under the terms of an Act of Congress of 1856 by which such islands, if certain formalities were observed, came to "appertain to" the United States. The occupation was not continuous, however, and since some of the islands were outlying members of British archipelagoes their status remained ambiguous. On maps, both British and American, they were usually marked as British.[26]

The desire to complete the "All Red" system of British cable communications round the world by a cable from Canada to Australia made the matter of sovereignty of some of the islands important. By the end of the nineteenth century Britain had laid and controlled most of the world's cables—an underwater empire still almost intact. The Pacific, supposedly so deep as to prohibit cable laying, long prevented the girdle from being completed, though the matter was agitated in Canada and Australia as early as 1877. As potential steppingstones for the transpacific cable, Britain annexed Fanning, Penrhyn, Christmas, and Suwarrow islands in 1888, and attempted to assert sovereignty over Neckar Island, an outlying member of the Hawaiian group. A proclamation of Hawaiian sovereignty over Neckar Island eliminated this last and badly needed steppingstone, and the present cable, laid and still operated jointly by the governments of Great Britain, Canada, Australia, and New Zealand rather than by a private company, was, when completed in 1902, carried from Vancouver to Fanning Island, a distance of 3,600 miles, without a break, the longest single stretch of cable in the world. From Fanning Island the cable goes via Fiji and Norfolk Island to Australia and New Zealand. The American Pacific cable, opened in 1903 by Mackay's Commercial Pacific Cable Company (a company three-quarters owned by British capital), presented fewer problems, since it could be carried from San Francisco via Hawaii, Midway, and Guam to Manila and Shanghai, with a branch from Guam to Japan; at Guam it also connected with a Dutch-German cable to Yap, in the German Pelew Islands, where

---

[26] Orent and Reinsch, *American Journal of International Law*, Vol. XXXV, pp. 443 ff.; C. Hartley Grattan, "Our Unknown Pacific Islands," *Harper's Magazine*, Vol. CLXXXII (April, 1941), pp. 523–532.

it bifurcated, one cable going to Shanghai, the other to the Netherlands Indies.[27]

In the years before 1914, particularly after the making of the Anglo-Japanese alliance of 1902, the affairs of the Pacific were relatively stable; Great Britain, the United States, France, Germany, and the Netherlands each had its spheres of influence and its possessions. The war of 1914-1918 eliminated the German possessions, German New Guinea being occupied by the Australians, German Samoa by New Zealand, and the islands north of the equator by Japan, which sealed the cable at Yap, much to America's disgust. At the Paris peace conference, annexation of Germany's former colonies by these countries was felt to be inconsistent with the spirit of President Wilson's Fourteen Points, though Prime Minister W. M. Hughes of Australia made a bitter fight to get German New Guinea for Australia. As a compromise, Wilson accepted General Smuts's suggestion of mandates in *The League of Nations: A Practical Suggestion,* as applying to the German colonies, and not merely, as Smuts intended, to former Turkish, Russian, and Austrian territories. The "C" mandate was created for former German colonies, under which the mandatory power, acting as trustee on behalf of the civilized world, was permitted to administer his mandated territory as an integral part of his own territories. This near-approach to annexation had perforce to satisfy the bellicose Hughes.[28] To Australia therefore, German New Guinea, New Britain, and the German Solomons were mandated; to New Zealand, western Samoa; to Japan, the Caroline, Pelew, Marshall, and Marianne Islands, formerly belonging to Germany. Thus did Australia and New Zealand, and also, unfortunately, Japan, join the ranks of the Great Powers controlling the islands of the Southwest Pacific.

[27] Scholefield, *op. cit.,* pp. 222-227; Leslie B. Tribolet, *The International Aspects of Electrical Communications in the Pacific Area* (Johns Hopkins University Studies in Historical and Political Science, extra volumes, new series, No. 4; Baltimore, 1929), pp. 155 ff.

[28] Luther H. Evans, "Are 'C' Mandates Veiled Annexations?" *Southwestern Political and Social Science Quarterly,* Vol. VII (March, 1927), pp. 381-400.

With Japan, the United States, having failed to get Yap internationalized, negotiated a treaty in 1922 giving to its nationals free access to the island in connection with the cable station there.[29]

The final processes of partitioning the southwest Pacific, until the present war began brutally to revise the peaceful arrangements of a century, occurred only in the years 1936-1939. This time it was steppingstones for Pan-American Airways' projected clipper service from Honolulu to Auckland, New Zealand, that caused a new scrutiny of the charts of the Pacific for unappropriated islets. In 1936 the United States occupied certain of the guano islands, Howland, Baker, and Jarvis, parties of Hawaiian schoolboys being landed from the United States Coast Guard cutter *Itaska* in charge of meteorological equipment. Britain, which also has a claim to these islands, did not protest this American colonization, carried out under orders from the Division of Territories and Island Possessions of the Department of the Interior. Other guano islands, however, Canton and Enderbury, the former with a fine lagoon suitable for seaplane landings, provided more of a problem. They lie within the Phoenix group, part of the British Gilbert and Ellice Islands; Canton was visited by H.M. Sloop *Leith* in December, 1936, and proclaimed to be British in the name of King Edward VIII; in 1937 it was incorporated in the Gilbert and Ellice Islands Colony by an order in council. In 1937, Canton was visited simultaneously by United States and New Zealand scientific expeditions intent on viewing a solar eclipse; subsequently New Zealand sent two radio operators there. In March, 1938, however, President Roosevelt by executive order put Canton and Enderbury islands under the authority of the United States Department of the Interior. A protest by Great Britain, supported by the Dominions concerned, led to negotiations and an Executive Agreement signed at Washington in April, 1939. Instead of another partition, it provided for another, if miniature, 'condominium'! Great Britain and the United States are to administer these tiny specks of land jointly for fifty years,

---

[29] Tribolet, *op. cit.*, pp. 231-236.

without prejudice to their respective claims. Thus did two empires agree over these tremendous trifles.[30]

The war has brought to the average citizen interest in, but not much more knowledge of, the southwest Pacific and its problems, which, so far as they are colonial problems, are part of a worldwide dilemma. British policy in Malaya, because it did not stand up to the pressures of war, for which it was not framed, has been condemned in ignorance of its true achievements and failings in time of peace.[31] American policy in the Philippines,[32] and Dutch in the Netherlands Indies,[33] neither beyond reproach, have, by the bravery of their soldiers, been raised above the level of discussion. Yet an understanding, not only of the processes of partition which this lecture has attempted to describe, but of the colonial policies pursued by the different powers which thus divided up the southwest Pacific, is fundamental to a sound approach to the problem of the future disposition of this area. If the war brings this understanding, as well as that careful study of the life and needs of the native peoples for which Professor Hoijer so eloquently pleaded in the preceding lecture, then perhaps the Pacific, in spite of its tortuous though hitherto peaceful partitioning, may begin to live up to its name, to the benefit of all mankind.

[30] Orent and Reinsch, *American Journal of International Law*, Vol. XXXV, pp. 443–461; Jesse S. Reeves, "Agreement over Canton and Enderbury Islands," *ibid.*, Vol. XXXIII (July, 1939), pp. 521–526; Grattan, *Harper's Magazine*, Vol. CLXXXII, pp. 523–532.

[31] Mills's *British Rule in Eastern Asia* should be read as well as Miss Thompson's slightly shrill *Postmortem on Malaya*, cited above in note 6.

[32] For the Philippines see Joseph R. Hayden, *The Philippines: A Study in National Development* (New York, 1942), and for contrast Florence Horn, *Orphans of the Pacific: The Philippines* (New York, 1941). For Samoa (New Zealand and American) see Felix M. Keesing, *Modern Samoa: Its Government and Changing Life* (Stanford Univ. Press, 1934), and Grattan, *Harper's Magazine*, Vol. CLXXXII, pp. 523–532.

[33] See Amry Vandenbosch, *The Dutch East Indies* (3d ed.; Berkeley, 1942).

# THE PACIFIC IN THE DIPLOMATIC
# CONFLICT OF THE WAR

---

ROBERT J. KERNER

SATHER PROFESSOR OF HISTORY
IN THE UNIVERSITY OF CALIFORNIA

*Lecture delivered April 19, 1943*

# THE PACIFIC IN THE DIPLOMATIC CONFLICT OF THE WAR

FOR THE first time in history the greater part of the Pacific is the scene of a war which is at the same time a world war. That it is the opening of a new era on the Pacific is beyond doubt. Whatever its outcome, this majestic ocean will not be the same as it was before this war. It will bring a new alignment of forces, to say the least. To say the most would be to indicate that the Pacific will become the center of activity in the future, whether as the scene of the greatest peaceful development in all history or as the world's storm center.

I

The core of the historical problem of the Pacific has been China, once its greatest power, the mother of Asiatic nations and of Asiatic civilization. Napoleon once said of China: "There sleeps a giant. Let the giant sleep. If China moves, she will move the world." The problem of China arises from the fact that the world passed her by and, as a consequence, she has been in the process of catching up with the rest of the world while aggressive traders and armies knocked at her gates.

She closed her doors in the fourteenth century; but the Russians established formal relations with her in the seventeenth century and were followed by England, France, and the United States and other Western powers only after the Opium War. From the forties of the nineteenth century to the Conference of Washington in 1922, the rivalry of the great powers, of which Japan became one, was centered on trade and, since the flag followed trade, upon political and military objectives. Just before the end of the nineteenth century China stood in great danger of partition and disappearance from the scene as a state. But the Boxer Uprising saved her from that fate: the people rose originally against the foreign Manchu Dynasty, but were shrewdly deflected by it against the "foreign devils." Somewhat terrified by this demonstration of elemental mass power, the foreign nations gave up partition for mastery through spheres of influence.

It was at this time that the United States acquired the Philippines as a base near enough to the scene of action and developed the Open Door doctrine. The Russo-Japanese War, in which Russia became involved in the pursuit of a dream of empire which might be called a "Russo-Chinese empire" based on the Buddhist-Mongol-Buriat church,[1] was a conflict over the fate of China in which Japan had the open alliance of England and the tacit approval of the United States. That attempt to monopolize China failed and for a decade the powers settled down to their usual rivalry, the delimiting of their spheres, and the mending of their fences.

The First World War brought to Japan her first great opportunity to monopolize China. While the great powers were involved in war in Europe, Japan presented in 1915 the notorious Twenty-one Demands which, had she been successful in obtaining them, would have given Japan the monopoly of China's fate. Under persuasion applied by the United States these demands were considerably whittled down. When the United States entered the war, she recognized, in the Lansing-Ishii agreement of November 2, 1917, that Japan had a "special interest" in neighboring regions, but not a "paramount interest."[2] At the Peace Conference of Paris and in the negotiations for the International Consortium further efforts were made to clarify Japan's position in China. Japan was to restore the former German interests in Shantung to China and only certain railroads in Manchuria were to be excluded from the International Consortium.[3] In the meanwhile, the International Siberian Expedition, one main purpose of which from the American end was to prevent Japan's unilteral control of eastern Siberia,[4] created a situa-

---

[1] R. J. Kerner, "Soviet Russia in Asia," in *The Renaissance of Asia* (Berkeley, 1941), pp. 124–125.

[2] Stanley Hornbeck, *The United States in the Far East: Certain Fundamentals of Policy* (Boston, 1942), p. 20.

[3] *The Consortium* (Carnegie Endowment for International Peace, Division of International Law, Pamphlet No. 40; Washington, D.C., 1921), p. 62.

[4] See R. J. Kerner, ed., *Czechoslovakia: Twenty Years of Independence* (Berkeley, 1940), pp. 56–62; idem, "America's Interest and Britain's Policy," *Pacific Affairs*, Vol. XI, No. 3 (September, 1938).

tion which with other problems in China and in naval armament were brought to the Washington Conference in 1921–1922. There, under the leadership of the United States, supported by England and France, an attempt was made to give China and the Pacific a basis of peace. It was, after all, a deal the essence of which was to give China a chance to work out her own destiny in peace by ending spheres of influence and freeing her from international bondage, while Japan by geographical propinquity and the 5-5-3 naval ratio was to have the advantage of favorable trade without fear of attack and without prejudice to duly acquired rights.[5]

This deal lasted barely a decade. During that decade China began her revolution and national unification with ever-increasing speed. Japan's internal problems continued to grow more complex, while China's unification threatened to dislodge her from Manchuria and possibly serve as an example to Korea. Soviet rule in Russia maintained and strengthened itself and brought with it a threat of communist revolt in Asia, at least down to 1927. England, the United States, and France became more absorbed in their internal affairs. When the great economic depression arrived in 1928–1929, they became still more absorbed in themselves. Soviet Russia was in the midst of her First Five-Year Plan.

Under these conditions, the militarist clique precipitated the Manchurian Incident in 1931 with a view to discrediting the liberal government in Japan, and they succeeded. They inaugurated the chain of events which led from Manchuria to North China and from there to South China, and then to the South Seas. The sources of this development, which in tradition may be traced back to Hideyoshi, who dreamed of conquering the known world at the end of the sixteenth century, and to dreamers and planners in the eighteenth and nineteenth centuries, of which Shoin Yoshida[6] was only one, were followed in the twentieth century by the authors of the Black Dragon and the Tanaka memoranda. The long-delayed

---

[5] Stimson to Borah, February 23, 1932. *New York Times,* February 25, 1932.

[6] Yoshi S. Kuno, *Japanese Expansion on the Asiatic Continent,* Vol. I (Berkeley, 1937), pp. 147–178, 300–342; Vol. II (Berkeley, 1940), pp. 213–237, 351–388.

abolition of feudalism as an institution, but not its spirit, the hothouse brand of industrial revolution turned into a preponderantly state enterprise and a war economy, the crucial agrarian problem—all these fed into a single stream: world empire by military conquest, and political and economic subjugation of foreign nations through state (not individual) enterprise. Individual Japanese enterprise could not have competed with the Chinese and never really did.

It was not enough for the League of Nations and the United States in parallel action to declare Japan guilty of violating the treaties based on the Washington Conference. Deeds—military force and quick action—were required; and these were not forthcoming, whatever the reasons. Nothing succeeds like success. Japan left the League of Nations in 1933, not only because she was found guilty, but also to have a free hand—which she soon exercised. The simultaneous failure of the World Disarmament Conference gave Hitler an excuse to leave the League of Nations and begin the rearmament of Germany. The failure of the World Economic and Financial Conference the same year showed the inability of the democracies to create effective solutions of these problems. In that same year, 1933, Mussolini gave the first orders to prepare for the Ethiopian conquest. Thus in 1933 three great powers, Japan, Nazi Germany, and Italy, began defying the democracies, which previously had largely determined the course of world politics and world economics.

In 1934 Japan denounced the 1922 Naval Treaty of Washington. By means of statements made by Eiji Amau, director of the Intelligence Bureau of the Foreign Office on April 18, 1934, and the Japanese Foreign Minister Koki Hirota on April 26, Japan now claimed the right to monopolize the Chinese problem. "Japan," said Mr. Amau, "is called upon to exert the utmost effort in carrying out its mission and in fulfilling its special responsibilities in East Asia.... There is no country but China which is in a position to share with Japan the responsibility for maintenance of peace in East Asia.... Any joint operations undertaken by foreign Powers, even in the name of technical or financial assistance at this particular moment after the Manchurian and Shanghai Incidents, are bound to acquire political significance." Mr. Hirota said: "Japan cannot remain indifferent to anyone's taking action, under any pretext, which is prejudicial to the maintenance of law and order in East Asia, for which she, if only in view of her geographical position, has the most vital concern." Secretary Hull three days later replied, to the effect that "in the opinion of the American people and the American Government, no nation can, without the consent of the other nations concerned, rightfully endeavor to make conclusive its will in situations where there are involved the rights, the obligations and the legitimate interests of other sovereign States." Sir John Simon, the British Foreign Minister, took the stand that "His Majesty's Government naturally could not admit the right of Japan alone to decide whether any particular action, such as the provision of technical or financial assistance, promoted such a danger."[7] We may conclude from this that Japan had openly embarked upon the second attempt (the first being in 1915) to monopolize the problem of China, that is, to give it a Japanese solution. That year the first rumors were heard of negotiations between Japan and Germany for a military understanding. In 1935 Japan began the political absorption of North China, Hitler openly abrogated the military and naval clauses of the Treaty of Versailles, and Mussolini embarked upon the Ethiopian conquest. On November 25, 1936, Japan and Nazi Germany signed the Anti-Comintern Pact, which Italy joined the next year. Parallel action, "common designs in foreign policy," similar methods and strategy—the now famous "one by one" rule of picking off intended victims,—these marked the arrival in the world arena of a new and powerful movement. Though ostensibly directed against the Third International, against which it suggested little beyond ordinary police methods, it concealed vague verbal, if not written, provisions for parallel action and for

[7] H. S. Quigley and G. H. Blakeslee, *The Far East: An International Survey* (Boston, 1938), pp. 285-288.

the redistribution of the territories and resources of the world.[8] These beginnings were the direct origins of the German-Italian military alliance of May 22, 1939, and the Triple Axis military alliance of September 27, 1940.

It was in this way that the Pacific and Asia, stirred up by the further advance of the Japanese in China in 1937, became involved in close and direct connection with events in Europe.

II

It appears clearer, with time, that the effort to transform the Anti-Comintern Pact into a real military alliance was accompanied by stresses and strains in German-Japanese relations. Above all other calculations, Japan doubtless insisted that the alliance must not involve her in war on more than one front. There were two possible fronts for her: the Russian and the Anglo-American. In the summer of 1938, because of her mounting difficulties with Soviet Russia over the Manchukuo-Soviet border in the district of Lake Hasan and Changkufeng, the fisheries, the last payment on the sale of the Chinese Eastern Railroad, and the oil concessions in northern Sakhalin, Japan believed the time for the transformation of the Pact into a military alliance opportune. At this time Nazi Germany was preparing the Sudeten coup which led to Munich, and hoped to keep Moscow neutral and to prevent a combination of states from coming to the assistance of the victim, Czechoslovakia. She declined.[9]

As a result, Japan was compelled to sign an agreement with the Soviet Union on August 10, 1938, which amounted to a diplomatic as well as a military setback in regard to the disputed questions. The actual military phase of the border dispute was temporarily shelved, to be handed to a demarcation commission, and the other problems remained.

During the strenuous Anglo-French negotiations for an alliance with Soviet Russia and the simultaneous German-Soviet discus-

---

[8] R. J. Kerner, "Soviet Russia in Asia," as cited, pp. 140–141.
[9] David J. Dallin, *Soviet Russia's Foreign Policy, 1939–1942* (New Haven, 1942), pp. 219–220.

sions for an agreement in the spring months of 1939, Japan put pressure on England to prevent her from permitting the Soviet Union to include the Far East in the projected Anglo-French-Soviet alliance against Nazi Germany. Japan did not want to fight Russia and at the same time England and France. On the other hand, England was reluctant to defend the Soviet Union in the Far East against Japan, which would have meant a second front for the British Empire. Doubtless the failure to get protection in their rear was one of the factors which influenced the Russians negatively in their negotiations with England and France.[10]

There is also the indication that Hitler was reluctant to make an agreement with the Soviet Union. Before he decided to do this, he revolved in his mind the idea of using Poland in an attack on the Russians (after Poland under his pressure virtually surrendered control of the Corridor, which meant losing her independence). In this combination, Nazi Germany and a dependent Poland, which was promised political overlordship of the Soviet Ukraine while Germany exploited it economically, would attack the Soviet Union along with Japan. Japan was approached on the transformation of the Anti-Comintern Pact into a military alliance. After much hesitation she declined in April, 1939, not only because she resented German efforts to end the China Incident but also because she feared that Hitler might become involved with England and France.[11] This might drag Japan into a war on two fronts, against Soviet Russia and against the Anglo-French combination in the Far East. The refusal of Japan to accept this risk doubtless influenced Hitler to sign a military alliance with Italy on May 22 and to beat the Anglo-French negotiators to a pact with Soviet Russia, which he did on August 21.

While these negotiations were going on, a real military clash

---
[10] *Ibid.*, pp. 221–224. See also Harriet Moore, *A Record of Soviet Far Eastern Relations* (Institute of Pacific Relations, 1942; mim.), pp. 73–74, for another view, based on denials that Far Eastern considerations were holding up the negotiations.

[11] Dallin, *op. cit.*, pp. 223–224; H. S. Quigley, *The Far Eastern War, 1937–1941* (Boston, 1942), pp. 81–83, 169–170.

between Russians and Japanese occurred on the Manchurian-Mongolian border along the river Halha, in which the Japanese came out second best and suffered heavy losses. It was a large-scale trial of strength with full military paraphernalia. Thus Soviet-Japanese relations were under an acute strain at the very time that Nazi Germany was signing the agreement with the Soviet Union. This could not help but strengthen the hand of the Russians in the Far East.

Thus it was that Japan, whose chief objective since the Bolshevik seizure of power in 1917, was the final military elimination of that competitor in Asia and especially in China, was surprised by events over which she had no control, and plainly showed her discomfiture. The Hiranuma cabinet fell, the Japanese foreign policy for some time was in complete confusion. The new premier, General Abe, stated that "the settlement of the China affair" was "its pivotal policy." Was Japan to imitate Germany and sign a pact with the hereditary enemy, Russia, or was she to make a rapprochement with England and the United States? She could not remain isolated. One reason behind her partnership in the Anti-Comintern Pact had been her desire to get out of the isolation she imposed upon herself when she walked out of the League of Nations in 1933 and denounced the Washington Naval Treaty of 1922 in 1934. One purpose of the Anti-Comintern Pact was to isolate Soviet Russia, and now it was Japan that was isolated.

As a result, Japan had no recourse except to give up a military solution of her disputes with Soviet Russia and to patch things up as soon as possible. In the fall of 1939 and early in 1940, Soviet Russia and Japan made several agreements (October 28, December 31, 1939, and January 2, 1940) which promised to delineate frontiers, arranged for the final payment on the Chinese Eastern Railroad, and began negotiations with a view to recognizing each other's puppets, Outer Mongolia and Manchukuo.[12] Nevertheless, they still glared at each other and continued to snipe at each other in the

[12] Dallin, *op. cit.*, pp. 227–230.

spring of 1940. Soviet Russia and China drew closer; Japan watched eagerly the Nazi spring campaign in Norway and in the Low Countries and France.

For Soviet Russia and for Japan, as well as for the United States, the defeat of the Low Countries and the collapse of France, in May and June, 1940, was to be one of the major turning points in history.

### III

We shall examine first its effect upon Japan. The immense triumph of Nazi Germany had presented Japan with the second great opportunity for expansion since she was shaken out of her isolation by the reverberation of the guns from Admiral Perry's fleet in 1853. The First World War had given Japan her first opportunity, and she used it in trying to make China a complete vassal.

French Indo-China and the Netherlands Indies were now virtually defenseless. The French fleet was immobilized. England stood with her back to the wall, fearing actual invasion. The Dutch Government had fled to England. Soviet Russia now faced a Nazi Germany triumphant in Europe. Italy had entered the war, and the Mediterranean had become a real war zone.

Undoubtedly, on the basis of prior information supplied by Nazi Germany, Japan began her diplomatic aggressions by indicating to the Netherlands Government in April, 1940—that is, before the Nazi attack,—that she was concerned about any change which might take place in the *status quo* of the Netherlands Indies. This was repeated during the attack. After inquiry by Japan, England declared she would not intervene and Nazi Germany said she was not interested in the problem. On July 18, hard-pressed England consented to the closing of the Burma Road for three months.[13]

On November 3, 1938, the Japanese Government had issued, subsequent to the acquisition of Hankow and Canton, a statement to the effect that "what Japan seeks is the establishment of a new order

---

[13] *Peace and War: United States Foreign Policy, 1931–1941* (Washington, D.C., 1942), pp. 89–90; Quigley, *op. cit.*, pp. 181–182.

which will insure the permanent stability of East Asia." Now, on June 29, 1940, Hachiro Arita, Minister of Foreign Affairs, stated in a radio address: "The countries of East Asia and the regions in the South Seas are geographically, historically, racially and economically very closely related to one another.... They are destined to coöperate and minister to one another's need for their common well-being and prosperity, and to promote peace and progress in their regions.... I desire to declare that the destiny of these regions—any development therein and any disposal thereof—is a matter of grave concern to Japan in view of her mission and responsibility as the stabilizing force in East Asia." The Japanese Government followed this up on August 1, 1940, with the declaration that "the basic aim of Japan's national policy lies in the firm establishment of world peace in accordance with the lofty spirit of *hakko ichiu* [the world as one family], in which the nation was founded, and in the construction, as the first step, of a new order in Greater East Asia, resting upon the solidarity of Japan, Manchukuo, and China."[14]

On June 12, 1940, Japan signed a treaty of friendship with Thailand which began a series of steps ending December 21, 1941, in the vassalage of that country.[15] About a week later the French Government was obliged to prohibit in Indo-China (under Japanese inspection) the transportation to China of gasoline, trucks, and materials. The Japanese fleet appeared at Haiphong on June 25. With France on her knees and under pressure from Hitler, Japan negotiated an agreement with Vichy on September 22 whereby France "agreed to afford in French Indo-China all such facilities of a military nature as are required by the Japanese army and navy for executing their campaign for the settlement of the China Affair."[16]

Japan would not have taken these steps in an entirely new direction—the South Seas—were it not that she was negotiating for a

---
[14] Quigley, *op. cit.*, pp. 114, 182. See also *Contemporary Japan*, August, 1940, pp. 1007–1008.
[15] John L. Christian and Nobutake Ike, "Thailand in Japanese Foreign Relations," *Pacific Affairs*, Vol. XV, No. 2 (June, 1942), pp. 195–221.
[16] Quigley, *op. cit.*, p. 185.

military alliance with Nazi Germany and Fascist Italy. The Japanese Crown Council had decided on the military alliance on September 17, and it was signed in Berlin on September 27. It had been under immediate negotiation for about two months, but it represented the end product of five or six years of scheming and endless negotiations by Japanese generals and admirals, a number of whom had designedly been appointed ambassadors in Europe. Before it was signed, the promise of the neutrality of Soviet Russia had been demanded of Hitler as a guarantee that Japan would fight on only one front, against a possible Anglo-American combination. This promise Soviet Russia supplied during the negotiations in return for Paragraph 5 of the Alliance, which stated: "Germany, Italy, and Japan affirm that the aforesaid terms do not in any way affect the political status which exists at present as between each contracting party and Soviet Russia." The Soviet Union agreed to coöperate to deflect Japanese energies from her eastern front, even as clouds gathered for her on the western front because of Hitler's immense triumph in France.[17] It should be remembered, however, that the tension existing between Germany and the Soviet Union after the fall of France helped to save England from an invasion.

The other provisions of the Triple Axis Alliance indicated that Japan "recognizes and respects the leadership of Germany and Italy in the establishment of a new order in Europe, while Germany and Italy recognize and respect the leadership of Japan in the establishment of a new order in Greater East Asia." The three powers undertook "to assist one another with all political, economic, and military means, if one of the three Contracting Powers is attacked by a Power at present not involved in the European War or in the Chinese-Japanese conflict." The term of the alliance was fixed at ten years.

Analysis of the details of this instrument indicates, at least in the official published version, that it was a defensive alliance and required an attack by the United States—against which it was directed before it became operative. It has been alleged that a secret clause

[17] Text, *ibid.*, pp. 296–297; Dallin, *op. cit.*, pp. 336–347.

or explanation gave Japan the right "to determine whether the United States was the aggressor." This view is supported not only by a version which stated that joint military action would follow "if any one of them might become involved in war," but also by the fact that during the Nomura-Saburo negotiations the Japanese declared that they would determine the application of the alliance, and by the further fact that Japan did attack the United States and was joined by the two other powers.[18]

In the Preamble the three governments considered it "the prerequisite of a lasting peace that every nation in the world" should "receive the space to which it is entitled." In other words, every nation should have its own "Lebensraum"—space for living,—which, of course, must be interpreted as meant for the three powers to determine. Over the years from 1934 to 1940, it has generally been intimated that so far as Japan was concerned her sphere lay east of India. The Alliance was in fact an agreement to divide the territories and resources of the world among the three powers. It brazenly called for a division of the world by a "plunder-bund." Its authors may have calculated that if the allies could intimidate England and the United States without a war, so much the better. It was an offensive military alliance, nevertheless. Later negotiations were to indicate an attempt by Nazi Germany and Japan to entice the Soviet Union into the alliance by offering her, it has been hinted, expansion in the Middle East at the expense of the British Empire. When that power refused, its refusal became one of the causes of the attack upon her by Hitler and Mussolini. Thus, indirectly, it was directed in the last analysis against Soviet Russia also.

### IV

Because Russia chose to remain neutral in the face of this danger and because England stood with her back to the wall awaiting invasion, the leadership against this combination in the Pacific, as well as in the Atlantic, fell to the United States from that moment.

---

[18] Text, Quigley, *op. cit.*, pp. 294-295; *Peace and War*, pp. 81-82, 133, 134-139.

Early in February, 1940, during the strange inactivity which existed at the time, Under-Secretary of State Welles was sent to Europe to find out if there was "any possibility whatever ... for the establishment of a just and lasting peace in Europe."[19] He returned with a negative result. The effort to prevent the spread of the war—as in the case of Italy in June—was fruitless. Germany and Italy were warned when France collapsed that the United States would stand by the Monroe Doctrine, which, as Secretary Hull on July 5 stated, "is solely a policy of self-defense, which is intended to preserve the independence and integrity of the Americas."[20] The transfer of French and Dutch possessions in the Americas would not be recognized. The Havana Conference of foreign ministers of twenty-one American republics, held during the same month, issued a declaration that "any attempt on the part of a non-American State against the integrity or inviolability of the territory, the sovereignty or the political independence of an American State shall be considered as an act of aggression against the States which sign this declaration."[21] This referred to danger coming from both oceans. The agreement to exchange destroyers for bases with Great Britain in September permitted the sending of relatively greater naval forces into the Pacific.

On the day of the signing of the Triple Axis Alliance, Secretary Hull said that "the agreement had been in process of conclusion for some time, and that the announcement merely made clear to all a relationship which had long existed in effect." He had previously told the French ambassador that "Hitler was out to become the ruthless and utterly destructive conqueror of Europe, and that the Japanese military clique was bent on the same course in the Pacific area from Hawaii to Siam." Three days after the signing of the Alliance, on September 30, 1940, he emphasized to the British Ambassador that "the special desire of [the United States] was to see Great Britain succeed in the war and that its acts and utterances with respect to the Pacific area would be more or less affected by the question what course would most effectively and legitimately

---

[19] *Peace and War*, pp. 69–70.   [20] *Ibid.*, p. 76.   [21] *Ibid.*, p. 79.

aid Great Britain in winning the war."[22] It was at this point that the United States began to assume the active leadership in the diplomatic conflict in the Pacific.

Because the United States was unprepared for a war on two oceans, prudence dictated that the concrete measures adopted should be in the nature of warnings and be restrictive, instead of entirely prohibitive at once in all cases. On the basis of the Export Control Act of July 2, 1940, the policy of refusing licenses for export of basic war materials was begun in August of that year. In September it was announced that the export of iron and steel scrap would be prohibited on October 16. When the Japanese ambassador, Horinouchi, protested that this might be considered an "unfriendly act," Secretary Hull told him this was really "amazing" after what Japan had done to American rights in China. "We and all other nations were expected by Japan to sit perfectly quiet and be cheerful and agreeable, but static, while most of Asia was Manchurianized."[23] By the winter of 1940–41, shipment of many strategic commodities, including aviation gasoline and scrap iron, had ceased. In an address on December 29, 1940, President Roosevelt proclaimed the United States the "Arsenal of Democracy" and, on January 6, 1941, in his address to Congress he stated the four essential human freedoms and declared that principles of morality and considerations for our own security "would never permit us to acquiesce in a peace dictated by aggressors and sponsored by appeasers." The President's budget message called for an expenditure of nearly $11,000,000,000 for national defense. The Lend-Lease Bill became law on March 11, 1941. The American people, the President explained, had demanded "a policy of unqualified, immediate all-out aid for Britain, Greece, China, and for all the governments in exile whose homelands are temporarily occupied by the aggressors." Aid would be increased and "yet again increased until total victory has been won." To all it was patent that we had assumed leadership in the conflict.

---

[22] Ibid., pp. 81–82.
[23] Ibid., pp. 93–94.

V

The next important event in hastening the conflict was the Soviet-Japanese Treaty of Neutrality, which was signed on April 13, 1941. In the fall of 1940 and the spring of 1941, Soviet Russia was the object of diplomatic rivalry between England and the United States on the one hand and the Triple Axis on the other. The fall of France had weakened the Soviet Union's position over and against Hitler, and, in spite of quick efforts to secure herself territorially, Russia was losing in the Balkans. England offered an alliance in case of an attack by Hitler and the United States offered freer trade by removal of the moral embargo, with the hope that Russia would not conclude a pact with Japan, but instead would keep her guessing. Although there were other obstacles to the success of these sporadic maneuvers, the real obstacle was the policy of the Soviet Union, which decided to go it alone. She would not ally herself with either group; she would try to remain neutral.

At the time of Foreign Affairs Commissar Molotov's visit to Berlin in October, 1940, and later, the policy of Hitler was to draw the Soviet Union into the Triple Axis, supposedly with a bribe for expansion in the Middle East at the expense of the British Empire. Stalin wanted to avoid a war with Nazi Germany, but he was opposed to entering the alliance. He probably judged that this would make a vassal out of Russia and that in the end the Communist regime would be liquidated in the embrace of the Triple Axis, when the latter began to demand raw materials, with hints that German experts and engineers would "assist," especially in the Ukraine. He did not wish to play the role of a Mussolini. It was this refusal to join the Axis, rather than the numerous points of friction and rivalry in the Balkans, that led Hitler to build up, while neutrality still existed, an anti-Soviet alliance of minor European states. In the last analysis, in Hitler's mind Russia must be an obedient ally or he would crush her in combat. He did not give up hope of alliance until the last moment. On the other hand, while Japan would have welcomed the entrance of the Soviet Union into the Triple

Axis, her purposes would be secured by a simple treaty of neutrality. Japan was impatiently waiting to attack the Anglo-American combination in the Pacific, if it should not yield peacefully all she wanted. Russian neutrality would suffice—perhaps it might even be better in the long run. She was, however, ready to partition China and arrange a division of spheres in Asia. But the Soviet Union knew the value to her of a fighting China at that time.

The Japanese foreign minister, Matsuoka, in his visit to Berlin in March, 1941, found out that Hitler demanded a speedy declaration of war by Japan against England, and advised him to make a pact with the Soviet Union. When Matsuoka returned through Moscow, he stayed long enough to sign the Treaty of Neutrality on April 13, 1941. After promising each other to remain at peace and to respect each other's territorial integrity and inviolability, they agreed that "should one of the Contracting Parties become the object of hostilities on the part of one or several third Powers, the other Contracting Party will observe neutrality throughout the duration of the conflict." A supplementary "Frontier Declaration" pledged the Soviet Union to "respect the territorial integrity and inviolability of Manchukuo," and Japan, that of the Mongolian People's Republic. The term of the treaty was for five years.[24]

This treaty relieved Soviet Russia in the Far East at a time when Hitler was beginning to threaten her in Europe. The Axis had determined on its grand strategy, which was to conquer the Near East and southeast Asia and join in the Indian Ocean. The Soviet Union had tried to block Hitler in the Balkans. She was either to become a vassal ally or go down in defeat. Two months later he attacked her, on June 22, 1941.

In view of the neutrality promised by the Soviet Union, the Japanese had forced the virtual economic alignment of Indo-China with the Greater East Asia co-prosperity idea soon thereafter, in May, but were unable to do the same with the Netherlands Indies. In July, the Japanese, after putting pressure upon Vichy, occupied

---

[24] Quigley, *op. cit.*, pp. 296–297.

southern Indo-China, including the naval base of Cam Ranh as well as certain air bases.[25] This overt act indicated that Japan was preparing to carry out her new plan of dominating southeastern Asia and the South Seas by armed force. Renewed pressure, diplomatic and military, was exerted on Thailand at the same time. These moves were an open challenge to England and to America in an area of great strategic importance—a pivot of power in the defense of the British Empire—as well as sources of rubber and tin vital to all concerned and especially to America. The Japanese had chosen—the die was cast.

In the meantime, Hitler's attack on Russia late in June, 1941, had caught Japanese public opinion unprepared, even though Foreign Minister Matsuoka declared, the day after the attack occurred, "Something must be wrong with the brains of those who are surprised."[26] Prince Konoye's cabinet resigned on July 17 and was reconstructed without Matsuoka. In all probability Matsuoka was given to understand at the time of his visit in Berlin that an effort would be made to bring Russia into the Triple Axis alliance. If trouble should follow, Soviet Russia would soon and easily be crushed. Japan could safely embark on her war with England and the United States. Hitler's attack on Soviet Russia had presented Japan with a long-desired opportunity to settle with her. It may be surmised that Hitler argued that this would come easily later. Now, it was necessary to destroy the British Empire. Japan was already embarked upon her new venture, which required Soviet neutrality. Perhaps, also, the Japanese navy played a predominant role at this time. The conquest of the region of the South Seas was its pet project.

While the outcome of Hitler's attack on Russia was still doubtful in the summer and fall of 1941, the Japanese Foreign Office decided to try to gain the new objectives in the South Seas without a war by negotiating an appeasement with the United States.

[25] *Ibid.*, pp. 183–191.
[26] Dallin, *op. cit.*, pp. 349, 337–353.

## VI

In August, 1941, President Roosevelt and Prime Minister Churchill met at sea and announced in the Atlantic Charter their agreement on vital points of policy which were to become the basis of world peace. It was agreed to take "parallel action in warning Japan against new moves of aggression." A joint message was sent to Stalin offering coöperation in sending needed supplies. Exploratory conversations among President Roosevelt, Secretary Hull, and Ambassador Nomura to find a basis of agreement, doubtful as that seemed, took on a more serious aspect as the spring turned into summer and the Japanese advanced with armed forces into southern Indo-China, where they no longer had the excuse that they were directly fighting China. Japan charged "encirclement" by England, the United States, China, and the Netherlands, and we charged the Japanese in southern Indo-China with preparations for further conquest in a new area. On July 24, President Roosevelt offered, should Japan withdraw her forces from Indo-China, to secure a binding agreement from China, Great Britain, and the Netherlands neutralizing that region.[27] We had permitted oil to be sold to Japan, although public opinion opposed it, so as not to give Japan a pretext to move against the Netherlands Indies. Nevertheless, because of Japan's move into southern Indo-China, the United States, as well as other interested countries, had decided on July 26 to freeze Japanese assets, the effect of which action would soon cause trade between Japan and these countries to cease.

On August 6 the Japanese answered President Roosevelt's proposal to neutralize Indo-China by "disregarding" it, and asked for a special status there. After the settlement of the China Incident, troops in that area would be withdrawn. Secretary Hull informed the Japanese that Japan's counterproposal could not be regarded as "responsive" to the President's proposal.[28] The Japanese suggestion that President Roosevelt and Prime Minister Prince Konoye should confer was met with the American countersuggestion that agree-

[27] *Peace and War*, pp. 119–121.
[28] *Ibid.*, p. 122.

ment in principle on the main issues should precede it. On August 17, because Japan continued her military activities with a view to the complete occupation of Indo-China, President Roosevelt handed Ambassador Nomura a document in which it was stated that the Government of the United States "finds it necessary to say to the Government of Japan that if the Japanese Government takes any further steps in pursuance of a policy or a program of military domination, by force or threat of force, of neighboring countries, the Government of the United States will be compelled to take immediately any and all steps which it may deem necessary toward safeguarding the legitimate rights and interests of the United States and American nationals and toward insuring the safety and security of the United States." This was a stiff warning to Japan. The Japanese were also informed that if they would suspend "their expansionist activities and embark upon a peaceful program in the Pacific, the United States would consider resumption of the informal exploratory discussions."[29]

In his reply of September 3 to Prince Konoye's message of August 28, urging a meeting as soon as possible, President Roosevelt repeated the four principles which the United States regarded as fundamental and preliminary to such a meeting: "respect for the territorial integrity and sovereignty of each and all nations; support of the principle of noninterference in the affairs of other countries; support of the principle of equality, including equality of commercial opportunity; and nondisturbance of the *status quo* in the Pacific, except as the *status quo* might be altered by peaceful means."[30]

In the discussions before and after October 17, when the Konoye Cabinet fell, Japan refused to withdraw her troops from Indo-China, to abandon the Triple Axis (although she stated she would independently decide on its operation), and to withdraw her armed forces from China until she should have made a victor's peace, during which time the United States was not to help the

---
[29] *Ibid.*, pp. 123–124.   [30] *Ibid.*, pp. 124–126.

Government of Chiang Kai-shek.[31] Because this basis was unacceptable to the United States, the Konoye Cabinet resigned and was succeeded by that of General Tojo.

Mr. Saburo Kurusu was sent early in November to assist Ambassador Nomura. It became apparent very soon after the discussions were resumed on November 17 that he had no new plans or proposals, but that he hoped to secure a *modus vivendi*,[32] a temporary makeshift, to tide over "the present abnormal situation" until after the termination of the Sino-Japanese conflict, when a more liberal policy might be adopted. The conferees went over the old ground and maintained their positions. On November 26 the United States presented as a basis for future conversations a full statement of its principles and concrete proposals for a peaceful solution of the problems involved, all of which it had carefully stated in the previous discussions. It included only one unilateral commitment requested of Japan, to the effect that she "withdraw all military, naval, air and police forces from China and Indo-China." It did not include a request that Japan leave the Triple Axis alliance, but asked that "no agreement which either had concluded with any third Power or Powers should be interpreted by it in a way to conflict with the fundamental purpose of this proposed agreement."[33] Mr. Kurusu said that his Government "would throw up its hands" and consider the negotiations at an end when it received the memorandum.[34] On December 1, Secretary Hull told the Japanese envoys that we could not "sit still" while Japanese troop movements in Indo-China continued, because we were not sure what the Japanese military leaders would do. "We would not allow ourselves to be driven out of the Pacific." "There was no reason for a conflict between the United States and Japan. ... Japan did not have to use a sword to gain a 'seat at the head of the table.'"[35] President Roosevelt sent a special message to the Emperor of Japan, in the hope that peace was still possible.

[31] *Ibid.*, pp. 127–128.
[32] *Ibid.*, pp. 131–133.
[33] Text, Quigley, *op. cit.*, pp. 312–317.
[34] *Peace and War*, p. 137.
[35] *Ibid.*, p. 139.

While Japanese bombs were falling on the American fleet at Pearl Harbor, the Japanese envoys handed to Secretary Hull a memorandum which was regarded as Japan's answer to the United States memorandum of November 26 and to President Roosevelt's message of December 6 to the Emperor of Japan. In it the United States was accused of obstructing "the establishment of a general peace between China and Japan," of attempting to "frustrate Japan's aspiration to the ideal of common prosperity in coöperation with these regions," of failing to show "in the slightest degree a spirit of conciliation," of "scheming for the extension of the war," and of "aiding Great Britain and preparing to attack, in the name of self-defense, Germany and Italy, two powers ... striving to establish a new order in Europe," etc. Whereupon Secretary Hull said: "I have never seen a document that was more crowded with infamous falsehoods and distortions—infamous falsehoods and distortions on a scale so huge that I never imagined until today that any Government on this planet was capable of uttering them."[36] By December 11 the United States was at war with all the members of the Triple Axis.

What Japan wanted was to repeat without armed opposition in that strategic area of southeastern Asia and the South Seas what she had already done in China. This would not only have broken the British Empire in two, but would have constituted a serious menace to the entire Pacific. In this connection Secretary Hull had told the British ambassador in August that the Japanese plan was "to invade by force the whole of the Indian Ocean and the islands and continents adjacent thereto, isolating China, sailing across probably to the mouth of the Suez Canal, to the Persian Gulf oil area, to the Cape of Good Hope area, thereby blocking by a military despotism the trade routes and supply sources to the British." "This ... would, perhaps, be more damaging to British defense in Europe than any other step short of a German crossing of the Channel."[37]

---
[36] *Ibid.*, pp. 141–142. For text see Quigley, *op. cit.*, pp. 317–324.
[37] *Peace and War*, p. 123.

## VII

The year 1942 witnessed the signing, on January 1, of the Declaration of twenty-six nations, including the Soviet Union, giving adherence to the Atlantic Charter. "Each government pledges itself," so reads the first article, "to employ its full resources, military or economic, against the members of the Tripartite Pact and its adherents with which such government is at war." They also pledged themselves not to conclude separate treaties of peace.[38] Thus was created, in reality, the United Nations Alliance. On May 26 the Anglo-Soviet Alliance, with a term of twenty years, drawn up largely with the Atlantic Charter as a basis, was signed,[39] and this was followed by Lend-Lease agreements between the United States and England, the Soviet Union, China, and other United Nations.

A new development occurred in the Pacific when there came into power in Australia on October 7, 1941, the Labor government under Prime Minister John Curtin, with Dr. Herbert V. Evatt as Minister of External Affairs. An independent Pacific point of view was at once the outcome. Australia opposed the appeasement of Japan and advocated coöperation with China and Russia. A separate declaration of war against Japan, at once approved by the King, was issued after the attack on Pearl Harbor. Australia insisted on the leadership of the United States in the Pacific and on the creation of a Pacific War Council, which was set up in London on February 6, 1942. It was at Australia's suggestion that General MacArthur was called to Australia on February 23, not only to defend that part of the Pacific but ultimately to lead the offensive. On March 30, with New Zealand's active coöperation and after General MacArthur's arrival in Australia, President Roosevelt announced the creation of a Pacific War Council in Washington, consisting of the United States, Australia, New Zealand, China, the Netherlands, Canada, and England. It has been Australia's policy—

[38] *War and Peace Aims* (Special Supplement, No. 1, to the *United Nations Review*, January 30, 1943), p. 116.
[39] *Ibid.*, pp. 128–129. See also R. J. Kerner, "Russia and the Coming Victory," *California Monthly*, March, 1943, and Dallin, *op. cit.*, pp. 388–415.

and in fact that of the Pacific War Council—since then to have the Pacific recognized as an important theater of war and Australia, in addition to India and China, as a base for an offensive.[40]

### VIII

If, now, we look back to see what has happened, we note that the course of events in the Pacific since the Opium War (1840-1842) has centered on the problem of China, which a half century later began to modernize herself in order to catch up with the leading Western nations. On the verge of disintegration, China was saved in 1901 by an elemental mass movement, known as the Boxer Uprising, which the foreign Manchu Dynasty deflected from itself against the foreigners.

In the events which culminated in the Russo-Japanese War in 1904, the Russian scheme to monopolize the fate of China collapsed.

The First World War gave Japan her *first* great opportunity to give the Chinese problem a Japanese solution, that is, to make China Japan's vassal in one operation. This was prevented under the leadership of the United States. The Washington Conference in 1922 liberated China from this predicament and gave Japan naval security in the western Pacific, on the condition that she exercise in China only her natural advantages in trade.

The depression and the events leading to the Second World War gave Japan her *second* great opportunity to monopolize the fate of China, this time by definite stages, beginning with Manchuria in 1931, and then proceeding to North China in 1935, and South China in 1937. After the outbreak of the Second World War and after the signing of the Triple Axis Alliance in September, 1940, with the neutrality of Soviet Russia assured in April, 1941, Japan began to extend her rule to southeastern Asia and the southwestern Pacific—

---

[40] G. W. Warneck, "Australia in the United Nations," *Pacific Affairs*, Vol. XV, No. 2 (June, 1941), pp. 133-155. See also *War and Peace in the Pacific* (Institute of Pacific Relations, New York, 1943), pp. 48-62, and the studies by K. H. Bailey, W. D. Forsyth, Julius Stone, H. Belshaw, Charles O. van der Plas, and G. H. C. Hart indicated on pp. 137-144.

a process which Secretary Hull aptly called "Manchurianization." It was at this point that the war in Europe and on the Atlantic merged with that in Asia and the Pacific. This challenged not only the existence of the British and Dutch empires, while England was holding the fort alone, but the security of the United States on the Pacific, as well as of the basic sources of the supply of rubber and tin.

To "Manuchurianize" Asia and the Pacific was the objective of the military clique which dominated the Japanese government as a part of its program of world domination and as a partner in the Triple Axis alliance. With Nazi Germany and Fascist Italy threatening the Atlantic and the Mediterranean, aiming to "Manchurianize" Europe, Africa, and western Asia and attacking Soviet Russia at the same time, the United States was confronted with the greatest menace in all its existence. The policy of appeasement or conciliation had failed utterly to keep the peace. It had brought before us the choice of consenting to a new order in Europe, Asia, and Africa which threatened our very existence as an independent state, or of leading the conflict to destroy the Triple Axis.

The world will not be the same after this war as it was before it. Whether it is to be a peaceful world will be determined by the peace. One central fact, however, is certain. If China is not allowed to modernize herself in peace, she will remain in the future, as she has been since 1840, the storm center in Asia and on the Pacific. The fate of southeastern Asia and the southwestern Pacific is bound up with that of China. There can be no peace on the Pacific under such conditions.

NOTE: Since this lecture was given, on April 19, 1943, the United States Government Printing Office has published *Peace and War: United States Foreign Policy, 1931–1941* (Washington, D.C., 1943; 874 pp). This is the complete publication, including documents, of *Peace and War* (1942) cited in note 13 above. In *Papers Relating to the Foreign Relations of the United States. Japan: 1931–1941* (2 vols.; Washington, D.C., 1943) numerous other documents are to be found. Examination of these materials has not revealed any conclusions which require revision of the original lecture.

# STRATEGY

---

### WILLIAM C. BARKER
PROFESSOR OF NAVAL SCIENCE AND TACTICS
IN THE UNIVERSITY OF CALIFORNIA

*Lecture delivered April 26, 1943*

# STRATEGY

THE TERM "strategy" in its original and literal sense means "the art of the general" (the Greek *strategos*). But no military term, perhaps no technical term of any kind, has undergone more changes of meaning, suffered more attempts to reach a standard definition, or been more diversely interpreted.

Whereas the term has, down even to modern times, been generally employed in a strict military sense, we have in the last century greatly extended the scope of its application to include the peacetime labors of nations in the field of stratecraft, that is, international politics. I think, in fact, we may logically separate the general subject of strategy into two parts: (1) statecraft, the *Weltpolitik* of the Germans; and (2) military strategy, the *Conduit de la guerre* of the French. The second phase is of course simply a continuation of the first; it follows when statecraft or diplomacy has failed to gain the objectives of a nation's foreign policy.

We may in this latter concept point out the greater relative importance of statecraft over military strategy, inasmuch as, if diplomacy is successful in its attempt to settle international problems, there need not be resort to war. Such a happy and idealistic state of affairs has been the dream and hope of man for generations. In fact, we hear much today of "winning the peace," and this implies some form of international plan—a control over those elements which through the years have been responsible for international misunderstandings and wars. Such a plan, if only partially successful, would indeed exemplify strategy of a high order.

Strategy in times of peace, or statecraft, needs for its potency—or at least has needed thus far—the passive power of the military. It seems that diplomacy's principal weapon has usually been the war instruments in the background, the silent threat of armies and navies, the "big stick" of Theodore Roosevelt. I know of few, if any, occasions when a weak military nation, although a sovereign state in the international sense, has been able to negotiate successfully with a strong power when the latter's interests are deeply involved. From this consideration we have, consequently, the close relationship in the past between diplomacy and the military. One point of view is that this interrelationship is provocative of war—that the military in the background forces the hand of diplomacy, either deliberately or passively. The answer to this contention may never be known. The peace deliberations following the current war will certainly have this problem to solve: how to preserve a continuous peace, with or without the contemporary existence of the material instrumentalities of war. Can international peace be achieved and preserved in the total or even partial absence of the agencies of war? In this connection I recall some comment following the World War I to the effect that man would soon come to his senses when he fully realized and evaluated the deadly and destructive weapons of war then in use and in prospect. The airplane with its possibilities was considered to be the instrument which would end war, inasmuch as it appeared to introduce into warfare such devastating man-killing potentialities. However, in the light of current world events we must reluctantly conclude that the more deadly the weapons of war become the more susceptible man is, under our present international system, or lack of it, to resort to the sword in settlement of his disagreements with his fellow men.

I do not propose to discuss our own national strategy immediately prior to Pearl Harbor; that is dangerous ground for a military man. However, I may mention, as of historical interest in connection with statecraft's part in the events preceding war the very erratic and timid policy of the Chamberlain ministry in England. It is generally agreed that, though Chamberlain's efforts were unduly conciliatory even to the point of servility, he did not have in his negotiations the instrument most necessary to courageous and aggressive deliberations, that is, sufficiency of military preparation. Without this backing, any discussions with Hitler were simply a waste of time, since Hitler then held all the cards.

A comparatively modern instance of successful statecraft without the moral support of military power was the courageous stand taken by President Grover Cleveland in the Venezuelan affair in 1893. With practically no navy or army behind his words, Cleveland recorded a signal success when he concluded with honor, and even with increase of prestige, a satisfactory agreement with England, the mightiest of the naval powers. A real threat against the Monroe Doctrine was skillfully parried.

We say that war is the last resort when other means have failed. This might be better worded by stating that war is the customary resort when the foreign ministry in power, or head of state, fails in the employment of its principal weapon, negotiation. Statecraft may expect to succeed in proportion as its existing agencies are successful in the use of diplomatic means. Who can say what another premier than Chamberlain might have done at Munich? On individuals in the saddle at the time depends the peace, maybe, of the world. The instrument, diplomacy, may or may not be skillfully employed. Individuals, not circumstances, mark the milestones of history.

The strength of the military power, its readiness for action, and the facilities for its expansion are naturally factors which must be considered in our foreign policy. In fulfilling its role of readiness the Navy prepares so-called war plans, and keeps these plans up to date. These plans are based on war with every possible enemy or combination of enemy powers. This phase of the Navy's peacetime function is sometimes misunderstood. Preparation of war plans has been interpreted by some individuals and pacifistic groups as positive evidence of the Navy's intentions to provoke a war. I recall hearing a member of Congress some time ago declaim with considerable feeling that such was the Navy's design, for he had discovered that plans for a war with a certain power were actually being drawn up, and if the Navy were not guilty of provoking this war why were plans in great detail ready for such an eventuality. Any open-minded person should appreciate that such studies are an important part of military preparation and peacetime strategy, and that a Navy which was not fully sensible of this responsibility would be culpably remiss in one of its primary functions.

With further reference to this item of war plans as a factor of peacetime strategy I may say that the Navy maintains a comprehensive intelligence service, with representatives in every important world capital and with headquarters in Washington. The primary duty of naval attachés attached to our embassies and legations abroad is to secure the information upon which our war plans are, in large part, based. These agents in general are clever men who possess or develop techniques for obtaining military intelligence. In fact, the foreign service as a whole is in effect a great spy system, clothed in a certain respectability of form and procedures. A sort of reciprocal understanding exists among the powers whereby an exchange of information goes on. If we desire certain important naval data from a foreign power and are unable to obtain it in the usual manner, we pay a certain price for it, we may say, by giving in return some information considered equally important to that power. Horse trading has more than one meaning. The desideratum, naturally, is to get the better of the bargain. Peacetime strategy assumes many forms and requires many and diversified skills.

Washington warned the young nation against permanent alliances, although the alliance with France, the crowning glory of Franklin's labors, was largely instrumental in our creation as an independent state. This distrust by Washington of foreign commitments was the beginning in the United States of the doctrine of isolation. This doctrine was a keystone of our foreign policy, continuous from Washington's day to the First World War in 1917—and even then abandoned only in the sense that we happened to be fighting a common enemy with England and France. Opinion was divided and bitter, in the years immediately preceding the current war, on this vital issue of isolation. It had been called neutrality in other days. The influence of modern communication and transportation had reduced in effect the dimensions of the earth.

Our terrestrial globe, with some of its areas so remote from our own geography, had never been regarded by us in the global sense now so generally accepted. A recent article in the press casually stated that some official had flown from Melbourne to San Francisco in thirty hours. The young men in uniform returning from service at the various fronts mention Iceland, Russia, Africa, India, and Australia as if they were in the next county. Short wave carries the human voice around the world. Aircraft have wiped out the barriers of distance and water. Our national strategy has undergone revolutionary changes. Following the war, every nation will of necessity reappraise its situation in the international picture on the basis of new and radically different concepts. The doctrines of isolation and neutrality will occupy a large place in the formulation of postwar policy.

The strategy of the Pacific may be dated from Perry's cruise to Japan. It developed slowly. Its real significance began to dawn on the Americas with the beginning of the century, and coincident with Japan's surprising military and naval successes in the Russo-Japanese War of 1904. Our Pacific outlook since that year has been for the most part confined to a watch on Japan, together with the formulation of strategy and plans for what appeared to be inevitable conflict with a natural enemy.

Now statecraft, through its essential instrument diplomacy, may still continue to function in wartime. It may concern itself with relations with neutrals and nonbelligerents with a view to the continuance of their neutrality or nonparticipation. It attempts to prevent an increase in the number of a nation's enemies. It strives to gain allies. Political battles in the field of statecraft are being waged, in the current war, in Turkey, India, South America, and Africa. Decisions in these areas may have a tremendous if not actually controlling effect on the war. In proportion to whatever diplomatic successes may be gained in these "hot spots," just so may the use of military force be diminished, and such a success, even though minor on its face, may provide a contribution to final victory of the first order of importance. The statesman on a delicate mission of this character in time of war may actually swing the struggle from a military back again to a political contest. However, let us now confine ourselves to the strategy of the employment of the military resources of a nation, but always with full recognition of the potentialities of the pen and tongue, skillfully utilized by a trained, tactful, and experienced foreign service.

It appears desirable, before proceeding further in this discussion, to clear up some additional matters of definition. The distinction between strategy and tactics should be pointed out; that is, the distinction in the military sense. The terms are generally used interchangeably by other than military men. The dividing line is not clearly drawn: one merges into the other, both in actual employment of the material instruments of war and in the geographic areas of war operations. Modern instrumentalities of war, in particular aircraft and radio communication, have made the borderlines extremely indistinct until in actual operations one has difficulty in determining with any degree of definiteness where one of these fields begins and the other ends.

We may say that when the application of the military instrument merges into actual-contact fighting, the dispositions for and control of such direct action are termed "tactics." But the two categories, though loosely convenient for discussion, can never be truly divided into, let us say, separate compartments, because each not only influences but overlaps the other. At the War College we used to say that strategy embodied the field of operations prior to the contact of two fleets; on contact, the art of the actual physical employment of the combat elements of the fleets was known as tactics—in short, tactics in sight of your enemy, strategy preliminary to the sight contact. Strategy, called by some writers "grand tactics," comprises the combination and movements of forces preparatory to, and in readiness for, the battle, that is, the plan upon which the actual application of force as distinct from other agencies is to be imposed.

At the War College we used to conduct strategical operations as chart maneuvers, inasmuch as large areas were involved, sometimes the entire Pacific Ocean; whereas the conduct of the battle, beginning with physical contact of the fleets, was transferred from the chart to the game board, where a room of some 40 feet by 60 feet in dimensions might represent a sea area of some hundred square miles. This was a convenient device for separation of the two categories of operations, and particularly so since strategy and tactics were separate academic departments, so to speak, and when the strategy department had located the enemy, then the tactics department took over and conducted the combat operations.

Prior to the advent of aircraft into naval operations, we arbitrarily established this boundary between strategy and tactics as the instant of time when sight contact with the enemy was established. From an elevated observation station on a battleship, an enemy's masts, under good conditions of visibility, would appear over the horizon at a range of about 30,000 yards, say 15 sea miles. The art of maneuvering a fleet in sight of the enemy now came into full play—battle tactics then took over; the tactician was in charge, not the strategist, although both functions were, in general, embodied in the same individual, the admiral. "Commence firing" with main batteries occurred shortly after sight contact. Ranging salvos soon established the gun sight range.

Now when aircraft entered the picture we revised our concepts concerning this boundary or marginal zone between strategy and tactics. We enlarged the field of tactical operations to include the sea area covered by the tactical scouting of our planes. In reality, and as far as battle dispositions of the fleet were concerned, the contact was made as soon as the short-radius scouts supplied to the admiral the factors necessary to tactical operations, that is, location of the enemy (either geographical or relative to one's own forces), his speed, course, and the composition and the pattern of his disposition. The eyes of the fleet were now able to see hundreds of miles. The tactical area had been enlarged manyfold; in fact, as the square of the operating radius of the tactical scouts.

Furthermore as the range of our aircraft increased they were employed in strategical scouting. These planes covered tremendous areas in their searches. Then certain of the planes assumed combat functions; the bombers and torpedo planes with their fighter escorts and protection took the play, so to speak, away from the surface ships. They monopolized the fleet's job. Aircraft became not only the eyes of the fleet, but also its principal offensive weapon. The situation was now as if the range of the battleships' guns had been increased by several hundred miles. Aircraft have stolen the show so completely in naval operations that we now have the spectacle of a naval battle being fought from start to finish without the surface vessels of either our own or the enemy's fleet ever seeing each other. Such was the situation at the actions in the Coral Sea and off Midway in May and June, 1942. In fact, shore-based aircraft of both the Army and Navy got into the battles. And later, in the Bismarck Sea, shore-based aircraft alone destroyed a convoy and its naval escort.

Where is the marginal zone now between strategy and tactics? Aircraft scouting by long-range patrol planes may, if sufficient numbers of them are available and bases sufficient for their essential services are established, cover effectively the entire area of probable operations. From this viewpoint I can, without straining my imagination too much, envision the entire Pacific Ocean as a tactical area. Provided with continuous radio information from his planes, the admiral may have before him a chart showing every detail of his own fleet's and the enemy's movements, a picture just as inclusive and accurate as if he saw the entire Pacific area with his own eyes. The strategist, in the old sense, has lost his role. It is now tactics from the beginning to the end of the campaign.

As an example of the changing conduct of naval operations I recall a fleet exercise of some years ago in which a plane flew over the enemy fleet in the dark, dropped flares to illuminate the area, took a composite photograph of the enemy dispositions, sealed the film in a container, flew back to its own command, and dropped the container on the deck of the flagship, where the film was developed and enlarged and prints were placed in the admiral's hands. A detailed picture, not just a description, was thereby made available as an accurate basis for the admiral's planning. The picture could, through the medium of continuous information, be kept up to date throughout the operations. As a further development of this technique the information from the scouting forces is now sent in to the admiral in the form of radio photographs. The admiral keeps his principal subordinate units continuously informed of the changing picture by photographic radio transmission on ultra-high nondetectable frequency. My imagination again permits me to look into the future and visualize the modern admiral with his staff, comfortably seated in a soundproof compartment of a superplane, moving in the stratosphere and directing the far-flung operations of his command, air, land, surface, and subsurface elements, with perfect security and detached from the immediate noise and distraction of the actual combat. In fact, there is no tactical consideration which would prevent the commander-in-chief from conducting the modern naval campaign from a deep bombproof land headquarters. Such are the possibilities and the virtual certainties of the passing parade in naval operations, brought about by those two giants of modern science, aviation and radio communication. This is a far cry from the business of the naval officer of only a few years past.

There is a basic concept in war: "The objective should invariably be the armed forces of the enemy, wherever they may be." Organized military resources, that is, the armed forces of the enemy, must be eliminated or broken either materially or in spirit. The mere occupation of territory or of a sea area or of a strategic zone does not defeat an enemy. The military situation which has existed in the Russo-German conflict of the past twenty months might illustrate this point. To just what extent have the opposing armies and nations suffered in man power, in material, in productive capacity, in morale? These are the factors, still unknown, which will determine the outcome in Russia; not the movements back and forth across the wide terrain which has been the battleground.

There is yet another concept that has received considerable attention since Mahan's time. It is this: "It is the role of navies—that is, fleets—to control the sea." Control of the sea includes maintaining and exercising command of the sea. I must again refer to the influence in such a function that aircraft and submarines have played. When Mahan, our distinguished naval authority, wrote his epochal volume, *The Influence of Sea Power on History,* he knew nothing of the aircraft weapon and little of the submarine; these instrumentalities were as yet unborn, except as a dream or scientific possibility. He spoke of surface navies, and of the two recognized functions of a navy, observation and combat, only in terms of the cruiser (the modern frigates) and battleships. As late as 1908, when our Fleet made its historic cruise around the world, it consisted only of battleships and a few destroyers. The submarine and the airplane were yet to enter the picture as the dominating elements of a navy. Germany has made no pretense, in the current war, of control of any area by surface vessels alone. She has, however, given the Allies their greatest concern in the Atlantic with her immense submarine resources, and in the Mediterranean with her aircraft. For the convenient employment of these deadly weapons Germany has a wealth of strategically situated bases. Control of the sea, in the sense understood by Mahan and his disciples, is now virtually impossible as long as the air and the subsurface medium of operations may be utilized by even moderate numbers of the modern tormentors of a fleet. This monumental change in naval strategy has justified such recent statements from military students as: "The war is now narrowed to a conflict between submarines and aircraft on the one hand and production of surface vessels on the other, this latter mostly in the category of cargo and troop transports." As a development of this changed situation in respect to navies we now are giving serious consideration to the super cargo-carrier of the air, a form of transport immune to the threat of the submarine.

Wars are no longer localized affairs. With two or more of the great powers involved, it seems quite unlikely that the whole world will not be drawn in. Such global war makes a pooling of allied resources necessary, and this necessitates transport of supplies throughout the seven seas. Transport versus submarine and plane monopolizes the picture. Transport by air accordingly will be forced into our war operations. The transition thence to general peacetime air transport in all its phases would follow as an economic development.

This speculation on the future of transport in global war and in postwar commerce is intriguing. I note some recent figures from government sources on the part that the service of supply is playing today as contrasted with its requirements in the last war. In 1918, five tons of supplies per year per soldier were necessary for his equipment and maintenance. In 1943, ten and one-half tons of cargo space for his equipment alone and eighteen-odd tons for his maintenance per year are required. The amount of shipping to meet this demand is stupendous, and when the appalling losses from submarine attacks are contemplated the task of supply alone seems utterly hopeless. The 6,000 miles of ocean from our West Coast to the operating area in the southwest Pacific and the 13,000 miles to Russia via the Cape of Good Hope and the Persian Gulf, conceivably under the submarine menace at all times and necessitating continuous escort, are logistic factors which no war of other times or studies of war even approached in their colossal dimensions.

All types of weapons are being employed in this vital struggle in which supply is pitted against its destroyers. Especially along those parts of the supply routes which lie immediately along the continental margins of Europe and Africa, attack from both submarines and aircraft is both continuous and effective. Great losses must be expected. We are told that the recent movement of troops, equipment, and supply, together with combat escort, in the current African campaign required 850 surface vessels, approximately 5,000,000 tons, half a year's output of the building program. These figures are beyond the imagination of most of us.

Let us contemplate one of the elements in these great supply efforts of the United Nations, the human factor. Aside from the soldiers and sailors involved it is fitting that appropriate credit should be given to that legion of unsung heroes, the crews of the merchant vessels which plow the seven seas, day in and day out, in bleak arctic seas, never free of the menace from the air and under the sea. Such vital and courageous service, cheerfully given in this dangerous transport duty, will be recorded by historians, let us hope, as one of the outstanding contributions to victory. It is my belief that the sacrifices in life and precious cargoes which are a daily part of this service will be minimized in great measure, should war come again, by the transfer of the supply task to the air. The submarine's teeth will be drawn; time and space required in these operations will be reduced; the air will become the medium of what is now the controlling element in modern war, that is, the function of supply.

In connection with this speculation on the changing scene as far as surface craft are concerned, it is interesting to note the modern German strategy of war, a concept formulated more than ten years ago. German military students evolved a philosophy which now appears fundamental in their plans in the current war. This philosophy has come to be known as the "around the seas" technique, "around" in the sense of encirclement. It is a plan whereby a nation with an enormous land force, largely in the air, plus great numbers of submarines, but with a small naval power in the orthodox categories, can hope to do battle successfully with another power or powers which possess large navies. The plan called for an answer to the question, How to fight a navy without a navy? The answer hinges in the very obvious fact that a fleet is of little value without bases from which to operate. It calls for the destruction or occupation of enemy bases by land and air power and of the stoppage of enemy sea-borne supply service by submarines. The enemy fleet is thus driven out of the sea area and its control passes to the land power. In short, control of the sea, historically a naval function, is disputed and conceivably won by land power. The bodies of Nelson and Mahan must turn in their graves at the impudent suggestion. Yet the idea is sound; Mahan could not conceive of it, for he knew nothing of the new instrument of warfare, the airplane.

Germany has followed this plan faithfully in her efforts to gain control of the Mediterranean. She has sought to send the Axis armies to cover the coasts of the Mediterranean and to capture the bases of the Allies and close up the two outlets at the east and west ends, the Suez Canal and the Strait of Gibraltar. This was the underlying purpose of the German campaign in the Balkans, the most spectacular phase of which was the capture of Crete from the air. Here for the first time in history air-borne troops, largely in towed gliders, accomplished a daring objective, amazing in its technique and coördinated planning. Air power defeated a combination of military and naval power. The basic principles of war may remain unchanged throughout the years, but the weapons and techniques of their employment are changing radically. The new instrumentality, air power, is bringing about a revolutionary revision of all military and naval thought. The assembly lines in our many aircraft plants are providing the determining factors in this war. If any American, or Axis agent for that matter, entertains any doubts concerning the ultimate results of this war in the nature of an Allied victory, I recommend he find ways and means of taking a look at the unbelievable production in one of these factories. I know of nothing that would discourage the Fuehrer more devastatingly than such a visit. His own ideas of air power and the "around the seas" theory of winning a naval war without a navy would undergo a considerable revision.

Let us examine, as major items of strategy, the naval missions of the participating powers in the present world war in, say, September, 1939, the date of the beginning of the conflict. By reason of her experience in the First World War, in which her best naval effort was confined to raids on enemy convoys, Germany certainly neither planned nor expected any fleet actions, nor would she seek with her enemies purely naval encounters of any kind except such as would be inherent in attacks against merchant shipping escorted by naval forces. Those of us who recall the critical and gloomy Allied situation in March, 1918, feel quite generally that German submarine warfare against merchant shipping had for Germany at that time all the potentialities of victory against the Allies and especially against England, dependent in so great a degree for her very life on the continuous arrival at her ports of shipping, bringing foods and warmaking materials. Germany's purely naval encounters in that war, although fought with great skill and some success, had no determining effect in her favor; in fact, Jutland, not planned as a fleet action by Germany, but brought about by detached events and suddenly and spectacularly developed into a major full-strength contact, was really the beginning of the end. Jutland, fought in May, 1916, planted the seed of disaffection in the German navy, and this feeling later was communicated to the army and eventually to the civilian population. Mutiny in a fleet, born of a conviction of the hopelessness of success, is a grim and destroying enemy, more deadly than military defeat itself. The Germany of 1918 realized this bitter fact. Hitler's Germany of 1939 certainly appreciated the lesson. And so it is a sound assumption to say that the broad naval mission of Germany in 1939 was—as it still is—the control of the marginal sea areas adjacent to Europe and Africa, that is, the type of control which makes shipping in those waters hazardous. Such a control, if effective, would cut England's lifelines of communication and deny her the basic constituents of her war effort. With respect to this assumption of Germany's naval mission we may well ask why Hitler, during the years of his building of his great war machine, did not build more submarines. He is now, rather belatedly, concentrating on such a program. My only explanation of this early lack of full appreciation of the submarine possibilities is that Germany is not and never has been a maritime nation in the true sense. Possibly Hitler favored aircraft too exclusively, in the belief that this new weapon contained within itself all the elements, strategic and tactical, necessary to sea operations. Germany's modern navy dates from Kaiser William's time, a late date in history when measured against England's long and distinguished record and tradition of the sea. Germany has historically been a military power, the word "military" being here used in its restrictive sense, that is, pertaining to land operations. In the assumption that Germany's naval mission in 1939 was sea control of the water boundaries of Europe and Africa alone, we must make also the debatable assumption that Hitler's plans at the time contemplated only the conquest of Europe and Africa—this notwithstanding the implications of world domination in *Mein Kampf*. We might even credit Hitler in this matter of naval mission with considerable foresight concerning the place of land-based aviation in the naval picture. With the coastal areas of Europe under his control, an eventuality which he took for granted as an early certainty in his plans, ideally located air bases in great numbers could be expected, to be used in coöperation and coördination with his submarines. The many such bases along the Norwegian coast have been a nightmare to the Allied nations in their problem of supply to Russia via Murmansk and Archangel.

Now as for England there can be no question concerning her naval mission in 1939. It was, as it has always been since Nelson's time, the control of those parts of the seven seas, or of those seas entire if circumstances should so demand, which might conceivably become theaters of operations in her great and vital responsibility of securing England's communications. England is by necessity a maritime power. A great navy is a natural corollary of such a nation's political character. For these compelling reasons every Englishman is sea-minded; scratch an Englishman, so the saying goes, and you find a sailor. The Fleet is always deep in the affections of the British people. The attitude of England toward her Fleet as contrasted with her feelings toward her land service is obvious to the casual observer in its unashamed partiality. The Navy is the favorite child, the service which keeps the flag on the seas and assures these island people of the essential means of existence. In England's greatest conceivable extremity, her loss of empire, she can with her Fleet, she feels, hold fast in her island fortress. The word "fleet," it must now be emphasized, implies the modern concept of naval power, that is, the embodiment intimately into its organization of the fleet air arm. Even under this concept of a fleet it appears now that the Navy, long the pride and joy of the Empire, must share the affections of the English people with the Royal Air Force, of which Churchill said so recently, "Never have so few done so much for so many." The R.A.F. today is England's first line, not only of defense but of offense as well. The surface navy doffs its hat to the winged ships of the air, which, unlike armies and fleets, have no limited areas of operation, but enjoy as their medium the boundless spaces of the skies, over land and seas alike.

Inasmuch as the foundation of strategy is the determination of a mission, it appears desirable in rounding out the naval situations of the powers in 1939 to comment briefly on the attitudes of some of the less prominent naval participants.

The French naval mission in 1939, that is, the broad purpose of her naval effort, was, as historically it has been since the acquisition of her African empire in 1830, the control of the western Mediterranean, with its guarantee of safe transport of man power for her armies from the inexhaustible reservoirs of French Africa. However, the collapse of France was so sudden and dramatic that the French navy was virtually eliminated as a factor of importance in the war. There is some possibility of the future employment of the remnants of the French fleet in the Allied cause, but no contribution of importance is likely. In any mention of the part France has so far taken in the war, note should be made of the traditional attitude of the French people toward their navy. Although France has long had a tremendous colonial empire, parts of it in almost every quarter of the earth, and although her position as a maritime nation is not essentially unlike England's, nevertheless France fundamentally is not sea-minded. She has never apparently understood or appreciated the influence of sea power. After the Polish campaign in September, 1939, and at a time when France was a principal belligerent, in whose reputed great army and air force and considerable navy England was reposing a hope of important assistance, France adopted what has been called a "fortress complex." She sat down behind her impregnable Maginot Line, which began at the Swiss frontier and ended "in the air" at Sedan on the Belgian border. France's military glory rests on the victories of her armies. Her navy has always been her stepchild. France accordingly has no naval tradition. From the beginning of the modern English-French alliance, an airtight defensive and offensive understanding, it appears that England was to provide the principal naval strength, whereas France's contribution was her really splendid army. The arrangement worked in 1914–1918; in the current conflict it failed miserably.

As one of the most spectacular military disasters of all time, and as one of the culminating phases of the short spring campaign in France and the Lowlands (May–June, 1940), let us refer briefly to the denouement of early Allied strategy on the Continent—and to the miracle of Dunkerque. The naval part in the withdrawal of the British Expeditionary Force was a major one. The role of the R.A.F., small but determined at the time, was likewise a vital one. The desperate and inspired contribution of civilians, particularly fishermen, to that magnificent operation has given a page to England's history worthy of her best traditions. The sea background, always a factor in England's life, emerged triumphant at Dunkerque. Beaten on land, scourged from the air, England falls back on the sea, and there she defies her enemies, whatever their power and resources may be.

Winston Churchill, the embodiment of the English character and tradition, in June, 1940, announced in the House of Commons: "The Battle of Britain is about to begin. On its outcome will depend the survival of Christian civilization." With grim and prophetic significance he added, "Hitler knows he will have to break us in this island home or lose the war." England's sea tradition arises in her hour of greatest trial to provide the inspiration for superhuman deeds.

On June 10, 1940, Italy's Mussolini gave France the infamous "stab in the back." Italy's entrance into the war carried with it many elements which were to affect profoundly the strategy of all the participating belligerents. Italy had, in the opinion of most military students, a fine navy and a magnificent air force. Her army had had in 1936 the experience of an active campaign in Ethiopia, and it enjoyed a fair reputation. Italy controlled a large part of the Mediterranean littoral, with some islands well located for air bases along the western routes to North Africa and the eastern portion of the Great Sea. Italy's naval mission, and in this expression we include her well-reputed air force, was the control of the Mediterranean or such a degree of control that the operations of her enemies within that sea area would be hazardous. France was out of the picture. The only other contestant for the great prize was the Navy and R.A.F. of Britain. Here again, England's long sea heritage was to provide the rock on which Italy's fleet was to founder. On the sea, the spirit of Drake, Frobisher, Hawkins, Howe, Hood, Jervis, and Nelson could not be matched. This long sea tradition could regard Italy only as an upstart in naval warfare. Her revival of the ancient Roman name of "Mare Nostrum" for the Mediterranean was impudent and unwarranted.

The Mediterranean has historically been the theater of many of the world's decisive battles. From the days of Carthage, Greece, and Rome to the very hour of today's struggle the Great Sea has provided the stage. In some reputable opinion this current war of the democracies against the totalitarian axis, or at least its European and African phase, will be decided there.

In June, 1941, Hitler launched his attack on Russia. We need give little attention to the purely naval aspects of the Russian campaign. Russia had considerable naval resources in heterogeneous types of ships, but she had no naval tradition whatsoever. He fleets were, and are, strictly limited in their areas of operations. The Baltic Fleet appears to be virtually immobilized in the Kronstadt region, making feeble sorties from time to time against German troop movements. The Black Sea Fleet has little more than a nuisance value, and especially so since the fall of Sevastopol, Russia's only base of importance in that sea. A third Russian fleet, based on Vladivostok in the Sea of Japan, is, under the current status of the Russo-Japanese agreements, without any military effect. Should Japan strike Russia in Siberia—and many authorities feel that the possibility is imminent,—the Vladivostok fleet would be in grave danger. No naval men entertain any very high opinion of Russia's navy. What Russia's naval mission has been in this war, no authority outside of Russia appears to know. From Japan's experience in 1904 with a Russian fleet at Tsushima in the Sea of Japan, I doubt if Japan is much concerned with any naval threat which Russia might present in the Pacific.

We are now, in our considerations of the strategy of the powers in our present war, brought down in general outline to December 7, 1941, a day which, as President Roosevelt said in addressing Congress, will live in infamy. Japan's entry into the war, together with our own formal declaration against the Axis, has made complete the global character of the conflict. The entire Pacific Ocean and every shore it washes is now involved in all the deadly implications of a Pacific war, a war which events of the past fifty years have clearly indicated as inevitable.

Japan, by her bold beginning, has gained many successes in the western and southwestern Pacific, accomplishments which in their suddenness and completeness have "outblitzed" even Hitler himself. That such so-called impregnable strongholds as Singapore and Corregidor would early fall to the invader were possibilities considered fantastic before their actual occurrence. Here we must give full credit to an organization of offense brilliantly planned, coördinated, and prosecuted regardless of minor setbacks. Japan's military operations throughout were essentially amphibious, and undoubtedly all services were employed under a common command.

The devastating Japanese raid on the Island of Oahu, which precipitated the United States in fact into the world conflict, was coördinated with a similar attack on the Philippines and with troop movements to the Malay Peninsula and the Netherlands East Indies. Carrier-based planes apparently constituted the raiding detachments. The technique of attack without formal declaration of war was followed—a practice identified with Axis policy. Such attacks enjoy the full advantage of the military principle of surprise.

Now what is Japan's broad military mission in this war? Believe it or not, it is the control of the Pacific; not just the western Pacific, but the Pacific area in its entirety, from the Bering Sea to Cape Horn, and thence to Australia and India, with complete domination of the land areas within that quadrilateral outside our own continent, and the ambitions of Nippon may even include North and South America within the Japanese sphere. We in the United States are prone to discount Japan as a first-class enemy and to regard her aspirations of Pacific domination as actually meriting scorn. Seventeen months ago that appraisal of Japan was understandable though not sound. Today it should be apparent to all that Japan is deadly serious in her mission of actual control of the Pacific. She is already well along toward a consolidation of all her conquests and full exploitation of the natural resources of the entire western Pacific. More than 300,000,000 human beings of various degrees of civilization and culture are now included under the Japanese control. If to this mass of man power and resources be added China's and India's teeming millions, more than half the world's population would be marshaled under the banner of the Rising Sun.

What is our own military situation? The United States, now a full partner of the United Nations, is in a war for actual survival, burdened grievously with the necessity of wide distribution of her military resources. Much of our Navy is required in the Atlantic for safeguarding the vital supply lines to our continental allies, in England, Russia, Africa, and the Near East. The mission of our naval forces in the Atlantic is accordingly the security of all categories of surface and air transportation. The major adversary is the submarine, and this weapon constitutes a real and disturbing threat. Disaster is continuously imminent to these vital convoys, not only during their entire sea voyage, but even after arrival at debarkation ports, while at the docks in the harbor.

In the Pacific the naval mission of the United Nations, and that means the United States principally, is, for the present at least, security of communications to the battle areas. The mission will soon be broadened to include control of the Pacific; this objective meets its identical counterpart in Japan's plans, and accordingly all the elements of a long and exhaustive struggle are present.

The United States is experiencing for the first time in her history the alarming situation of a war in both oceans, a military problem of considerable dimensions. The two wars are distinct in every factor except the nature of their origins. The all-over strategy of the Allied War Council, as it is involved in the prosecution of two wars in two opposite world areas, is naturally not a matter of general knowledge. The balancing of our resources against the respective threats in these two oceans calls for the best intelligence and leadership of the Allied powers. We must assume that those virtues are being devoted to the task in fullest measure.

In concluding this presentation on strategy I feel that a few words on the subject of the attitudes of the people and of the press toward the war may not be out of harmony with the broad concept of strategy. The press news is generally misleading; its overemphasis or playing up of our own successes, even insignificant ones, and its failure to evaluate, its playing down of, our losses and mistakes, is confusing and dangerous. I do not refer to press releases from government sources; I have in mind the paraphrasing of those releases by the press, the tendency to paint the picture attractively for our side regardless of the essential facts of the release. Calling names and making faces do not win battles. Reflecting this influence of the daily newspapers, the American people generally fail to appraise the military situation correctly—many of them do not want to. That we fight this war on high moral grounds seems to convince the man on the street that we cannot lose. "He is thrice armed whose cause is just," is a very high-sounding and sentimental thought. However, the opposite theory, that "God is on the side with the most battalions," still is sound reasoning. Personally, in a battle I would prefer the battalions to the justness of my cause. Napoleon thus commented on this hypothesis: "A good general, a well-organized system, good instructions, and severe discipline, aided by effective establishments of supply, will always make good troops, independently of the cause for which they fight." In effect, we must not discount, belittle, disparage, or scorn our Oriental enemy. Japan is a physical contestant worthy of our mettle, if not of our political and moral ideals. I would like to see a more realistic appreciation here at home of the extremely critical military situation which we face in every corner of the globe. This will require some stepping down of our ego; evaluation of events based on facts rather than hopes and wishful thinking should be the basis of our war psychology.

Of the eventual outcome of today's mighty struggle I do not hesitate to voice a prediction; and such a prediction is not based on sentiment, but on hard, cold, visible evidence, the evidence of the most battalions, which historically win wars. The productive genius of the American people will not be denied. The mines, the mills, the factories appear to have no limits to their expanding production. A visit to one of our neighborhood aircraft plants—and they are typical of our production genius—has convinced me. Combine these resources with the intelligence of our genius for design and management, add the courage and initiative of the men who operate the product in actual combat, and there we have the elements which, with the loyalty and required sacrifices of the men and women and youth in the homes and schools, should resolve the tremendous conflict into ultimate victory.

# THE PACIFIC DOMINIONS

---

### J. B. CONDLIFFE
PROFESSOR OF ECONOMICS
IN THE UNIVERSITY OF CALIFORNIA

*Lecture delivered May 3, 1943*

# THE PACIFIC DOMINIONS

Australia and New Zealand are small communities far away from the center of gravity in world economics and politics. They differ greatly in historical development and economic outlook as well as in their geographical environment. Australia is a continent, but most of the continent is desert. The population of Australia is mainly concentrated along the eastern and southeastern fringe of the land mass. In this region are found not only the great cities, but the mixed farming, the considerable development of fruit-growing, and the more extensive wheat production which spreads into the drier lands across the ranges. Behind the low mountain ranges that skirt the coast lie great plains upon which has developed the pastoral industry. It is this industry which has given the country its characteristic and basic export, wool. Great "mobs" of sheep—on some "stations" running into the hundreds of thousands—range untended on these plains, cropping the scanty grass and saltbush. This is extensive farming, involving heavy capital investment and risk but relatively little labor. Cattle ranches of similar proportions lie even farther from the population centers; but the vast area of the interior is mostly desert.

Australia, however, is also a country of high industrial development. Its scanty population is largely concentrated in the capital cities. Melbourne and Sydney have both passed the million mark long since. Adelaide and the other state capitals dominate their local environment. Not only is there a very complete development of the lighter manufacturing industries; heavy industry has grown, especially during the war, to a remarkable degree. Mass-production methods, already familiar in agricultural and pastoral operations, have been applied to industry. Precision tools and instruments necessary for the manufacture of interchangeable parts have greatly improved the industrial equipment. Costs of production are not high and industrial development has come to stay. The nucleus from which has grown the modern complex of steel, shipbuilding, machine industry, and even airplane manufacture, is the Broken Hill Proprietary, Ltd., a great corporation that established itself originally by exploiting the silver deposits of Broken Hill. There has been a double outgrowth of this enterprise. Nationally it has reached out into metal manufactures, and particularly into steel. Internationally it has enlisted the support of British capital in the development of silver, tin, and other base-metal ores in Siam, Burma, and Malaya. In so doing it has become a considerable factor in the world market for base metals.

One further development needs to be noted. The great economic depression hit Australia first and hardest. Even before the stock market crashed in New York in October, 1929, Australia was laboring in difficulties with its balance of international payments. A sharp fall in the prices of wool and other industrial materials foreshadowed the financial catastrophe to come. It struck Australia at the moment when the supply of new foreign loans was drying up, and at the moment also when one of the periodic droughts with which pastoralists must always reckon was wreaking havoc on the back country. Faced by this triple blow, Australia's overseas assets were heavily reduced. Imports had to be curtailed drastically. Lowered purchasing power also brought unemployment and distress within the country.

Out of disaster, however, Australia gained new strength. Statesmen, public officials, business leaders, and economists, meeting in a succession of informal and formal conferences, hammered out a plan of adjustment and recovery. This was a practical compromise between—or, more accurately, a combination of—deflation and inflation. Wages were cut; public expenditures were reduced on the whole, but selectively; bond interest was scaled down. These measures were carefully calculated so as to impose an equitable measure of sacrifice upon the major economic groups in the community. At the same time, the external value of the currency was depreciated so that farmers received more in local currency for the proceeds of their exports. Even more important, the Commonwealth Bank was transformed into a true central bank, and it proceeded to arrest the spiral of deflation by issuing new bills upon which the commercial banks could safely extend more liberal credit to business and agricultural enterprises.

Australia emerged from the depression, therefore, before most other countries. It did so because of a courageous and systematic cutting away of deadwood in the economic structure and because, together with that drastic pruning, steps were taken to equip the community with a flexible and independent system of national credit. Equilibrium was restored among the economic factors of production within the country and between the national economy and the outside world. Upon that equilibrium a sound recovery was gradually achieved.

New Zealand differs so markedly from its greater neighbor that it has always steadfastly refused to enter into federal relations with the Australian states that formed themselves into a Commonwealth in 1900. It remains an independent, self-governing Dominion. Its three mountainous islands lie 1,200 miles to the southeast of Australia, across a stormy sea. Indeed, a Canadian visitor once described New Zealand as "small islands entirely surrounded by a wide belt of seasickness." Regular, warm rains, distributed fairly evenly over the year, make it a fertile land suitable for small-scale farming and particularly for dairying. On the foothills and lower mountain slopes of the South Island are great sheep stations, not so large as those of Australia, but still of a considerable size. Between them and the specialized dairy farms of the rich lands that were formerly forested areas, lie mixed farms on which the dual-purpose crossbred sheep produces both lamb and wool for the London market while a dairy herd produces the butter that also goes to London but yields the farmer a steady cash income. The main exports of the Dominion are butter and cheese, wool, lamb, and mutton. The dairy industry has long been almost completely organized along coöperative lines with butter-and-cheese factories owned by the local suppliers operating on a scale of output approximately five times as large as that of the factories in Wisconsin. Efficient organization, coupled with high productivity, enables New Zealand in normal times to supply half the butter consumed in Britain. At present the price of this butter to the ultimate consumer at the other side of the globe is approximately twenty-five cents U.S. currency per pound, but the trade is profitable enough to yield New Zealand an average standard of living higher than that of any other country, even the United States.[1]

The rugged nature of the country and the long coastline have made for decentralization and have buttressed the dominance of the countryside. Four towns of roughly equal size have emerged, and many smaller centers, though Auckland has drawn ahead in recent years as dairying developed and Pacific trade grew in importance. Deliberate policy, particularly since the Labor government came to power in 1935, has aimed at industrial growth; but New Zealand still lags far behind Australia in this respect. It has not yet established heavy industries, and, with a population of little more than a million and a half, no iron ore, and rather inaccessible coal deposits, may have difficulty in doing so. Its great wealth lies in the efficient exploitation of its grasslands. More than Australia it bears the deep imprint of deliberate colonization. Group settlements were planted. Many of them were founded on religious and political beliefs as strong as those which left their mark on the New England communities.

Although Australians and New Zealanders are prone to stress their distinctive characteristics, and New Zealanders in particular object strongly to the word "Australasia," the characteristics they have in common are perhaps greater and more significant than their differences. There is much good-humored banter between the two countries. Their peoples are sufficiently unlike in speech, mannerisms, and even physical appearance to be fairly readily distinguished—at least in the more extreme types. They are at least as

[1] Cf. Colin Clark, *The Conditions of Economic Progress* (London, 1940), table and chart facing p. 148.

separable as citizens of Canada and the United States. Yet, in spite of their differences, they are alike in being people of almost wholly British stock, few in numbers, isolated in a remote region of the globe, directly menaced by the great and awakening populations of Asia.

In a very real sense, Australia and New Zealand should be regarded as outposts of British economic development and British culture. Their whole life is linked closely with that of Britain. They are fully self-governing, but they prefer to exercise their influence on world affairs as members of the British Commonwealth rather than as small independent nations. This does not mean acceptance of domination by London. They would repudiate any semblance of control by London over their domestic affairs, or any suggestion of interference. London would never wish to interfere. The Dominions feel free also at international conferences to express their own national views, which have frequently clashed with those of the United Kingdom. Australian and New Zealand cabinets, like those of Canada and South Africa, are "equal in status if not in stature" to the British cabinet. When the King visits a Dominion he is attended by, and accepts the advice of, his ministers in that Dominion. The Dominions exchange diplomatic representatives with Britain and with each other and also with foreign countries such as the United States. Their legations at Washington deal directly with the State Department, and are completely independent of the British embassy in every respect.

Nevertheless, the ties that link them in the loose association of the Commonwealth are very real. As a result of long political experience, some of it gained the hard way during the American War of Independence, the British people learned how to deal with the Dominions. They realize the wisdom of Edmund Burke's plea that "slavery they can have anywhere.... But until you become lost to all feeling of your true interest and your natural dignity, freedom they can have from none but you." In consequence, they have been rewarded, as Burke prophesied, by finding that "the close affection which grows from common names, from kindred blood, from similar privileges, and equal protection" are truly "ties which, though light as air, are as strong as links of iron."

Any discussion of the place of Australia and New Zealand in world affairs must begin from this point. They are bound irrevocably in love and loyalty to the British Commonwealth. Twice in a generation they have sent their sons freely to fight by the side of their British partners. What the Anzacs did at Gallipoli in 1915 and later in France and Palestine, their sons have outdone in the long and successful defense of Tobruk, at Mount Olympus, defending the pass at Thermopylae, and exacting a bitter price for the loss of Crete. In face of the direct threat of invasion of their homeland the Australian divisions in the Middle East were withdrawn, but the last of them stayed to play a decisive role in the great battle of El Alamein. Other Australian divisions have since fought in defeat at Singapore and in victory at Buna. A band of guerrillas is still fighting on Timor Island, as New Zealanders are still fighting in the mountains of Greece and Crete. A New Zealand division has remained in the Middle East. It was flung into the breach at El Alamein after the fall of Tobruk. Surrounded, and out of ammunition, it paid the price of cutting its way out with the bayonet. New Zealand and Australia have already lost more men in this war, in proportion to their population, than any others of the United Nations except Russia; but their divisions are kept at full strength. The New Zealanders have taken their share in the great campaign across North Africa and are at this moment attacking the enemy in the last range of mountains guarding the Carthaginian plain. The Australians have lost more men in the New Guinea campaign than were lost by the Americans.

The experience of these distant Dominions in the two wars has made them thoroughly conscious of the bitter fruits of international anarchy. Their first and unshakable loyalty is to their partners in the British Commonwealth. But they are determined in their own right, and as members of the Commonwealth, to replace anarchy by order in world affairs. There can be no doubt of the relief they felt when the naval, military, and air strength of the United States was extended from island to island across the Pacific to secure their line of communications. They have welcomed the American service men now stationed within their own territories, not only with relief and gratitude, but with real friendship and camaraderie. The conduct of the American troops has won the gratitude and affection of their comrades "down under." American supplies and equipment command the admiration and grateful thanks of these isolated and threatened communities. In return, the United States forces, not only in Australia and New Zealand, but in the Solomon Islands and New Guinea and even farther afield, are fed, and in part supplied, by reciprocal lend-lease. Admirable hospitals, barracks, and service centers are built for them. The total amount of reciprocal lend-lease aid to the American forces is impressive. The American forces have in turn built air bases, notably in New Zealand.

The Pacific Dominions are finding their destinies closely linked with the United States. Like Canada, they have developed a way of life and an outlook very close to the American. They know also that they must work increasingly with the United States in coöperative measures for security in the Pacific region. They would like to do more trade with the United States. American automobiles, refrigerators, and other manufactures seem very good to Australians and New Zealanders. They already buy them heavily. Each of these Dominions has a heavy import balance with the United States which it must settle through London. They are the heaviest importers per head in the world. They would certainly switch more of their importing capacity to American goods if they could get hold of the dollar exchange with which to pay. They are good customers in another sense also, since no loan has ever been defaulted in their history and their credit is good. To buy more they must sell more, and they ardently hope that in the pursuance of the reciprocal-trade-agreement program they may be able to negotiate agreements to increase their trade with the United States.

All this real good will based upon a common interest in Pacific security, and ultimately upon ideals held in common, should not be interpreted to mean a weakening of the ties that bind the Pacific Dominions to their partners in the British Commonwealth. Neither they nor Canada believe that the Commonwealth is in any danger of disruption. Indeed, it is stronger as a result of this war. And this is so because the main political effect of the war has been to strengthen their national consciousness. It may seem a paradox to say that an international association, for that is what the Commonwealth is, has been strengthened by the growing nationalism of its member states. But it does not seem a paradox to these British peoples, because they know that only in an international community can their nationalism grow to its full strength. They are ready, and indeed they are eager, to take their part in creating and maintaining a greater international community. They are deeply committed to doing so by the blood of two generations that has been shed in wars for which they certainly were not responsible and from which they had nothing to gain. It is their great hope that they may play their part, together with their partners in the British Commonwealth and with the United States, in transforming the war alliance of the United Nations into a permanent structure of world order.

After all, it must be remembered that they are a handful of people, far fewer than ten millions, facing the thousand millions in Asia across distances that shrink with every improvement in aeronautics. Even a generation ago their contacts with Asia and their knowledge of the Asiatic peoples were very slight. Today an industrialized Japan, schooled in the arts of war and equipped with all its modern mechanisms, is attacking at their very gates. Australia particularly, with the enemy less than two hours' flight away, is very conscious of its dependence upon MacArthur's bomber line. New Zealand is in some respects even more helpless, since her best fighting men are in Tunisia.

It seems obvious enough that such scanty populations scattered over a relatively great area and in possession of rich mineral and agricultural resources are in a very weak strategic position. Their great need is more population; but they have been adamant, as California has been adamant and for the same reasons, in shutting the door to Asiatic immigration. They have welcomed, and even assisted, immigrants from Britain, but the population of Britain is not now increasing fast and is aging rapidly, so that the stream of immigrants has dwindled. Few have found their way from continental Europe to either Australia or New Zealand. It would be good, though in some quarters unwelcome, if more could do so after this war.

Perhaps this is the most crucial issue facing the Dominions in the postwar years. They need to export their surpluses of food and raw materials, but above all they need to stiffen their own defense by adding to their man power. In the past the Royal Navy has been their shield. As long as Britain kept command of the seven seas they were relatively safe in maintaining a small population at high living standards. But Singapore fell quickly and the British Navy is no longer able to command the seas, particularly against hostile aircraft. Therefore Australians and New Zealanders, while hoping and working for collective security and for American aid, must see to their own defenses. To man them and above all to provide equipment for them, they need more people.

If their hopes of collective security fail, they will be bound to sacrifice also their hopes for maintaining the efficiency of their specialized production for world markets and with it their high living standards. They have come very close to being invaded in this war, and their safety still depends upon a very long lifeline that might become precarious if the United Nations were for any reason to lose command of the air. Unless they can feel reasonably sure of prompt and effective material support in any future emergency, they are bound to take precautions to equip themselves with automotive and aircraft factories and other means of producing the instruments with which to defend themselves. Even at the cost of sacrificing some measure of economic advantage and comfort, they must make themselves secure as best they can.

There is not much more that can be said on the economic and political outlook of these distant peoples who have been brought so close to us by the comradeship of a common war effort. They have fought a good fight and will be stalwart to the last. Many unfortunate and exaggerated rumors have been spread about the independence and defiant attitude particularly of the labor unions in Australia. It is difficult to resist the impression that the spreading of such rumors is largely malicious, the work of those who wish to impair the unity of the English-speaking peoples by repeating damaging statements about the British, whatever the origin or the accuracy of those statements may be. The worst of the rumors have been publicly disproved, but it is difficult to catch up with them all. There have been strikes in Australia, recently in New Zealand also—and one might add also in Britain and the United States. Labor is jealous of its bargaining position and exercises its democratic right of outspoken criticism. There is, in Australia and New Zealand, the same struggle as we have to preserve a controlled price equilibrium against the claims of competing social groups. Political conflict is just as vigorous; opinions and epithets are expressed just as freely and just as strongly in the Pacific Dominions as they are in the United States.

Australians and New Zealanders take these matters seriously and fight their political difficulties out in public, plainly and sometimes violently. But their record is clear. No peoples have given more of their blood and toil in this war. They will fight to the very end.

When that end comes, soon or late, they will do their best to insure that the catastrophe will not recur. They will do their best, but they are little peoples and it is the great peoples who will have the decision in their hands. The little peoples wait on their decision, and above all they await the decision of the United States.

Remote and little powerful as they are, these distant outposts of Western civilization are conscious that they have a pioneer role to play in world affairs. They are the latest and farthest outposts, the last positions occupied by the Western world in its great period of expansion. The Industrial Revolution was well under way before their were effectively colonized. American enterprise was approaching the final conquest of this continent. The network of world trade was almost completed. When the handful of settlers in Australia began to cross the coastal ranges in search of sheep pastures, and even smaller bands were consolidating their precarious footholds in New Zealand, the battle of free trade was won in Britain and the great nineteenth-century expansion was well launched.

From the very first the settlers in these new lands were conscious of their destiny. The first missionary bishop of the Anglican Church rejoiced in the error by which his diocese was defined as extending north of the equator. The first white blood shed in the Solomons and New Guinea was the blood of martyrs.

From the first days of settlement also, especially in New Zealand, there were men of vision who foresaw the development of the commonwealth. In 1852, barely two years after the founding of Canterbury, its first Superintendent, Godley, speaking at Lyttelton, pleaded for a form of federation. The six colonies of Australia and the six provinces of New Zealand were quick to claim, and Britain was ready to concede, the self-government that had been granted to Canada.

It was not long before the colonies became insistent upon their right to establish their own outposts of security in the Pacific islands. Other countries had followed close upon Britain in industrial development. In the 1870's, Germany began to reach out for footholds in China and island possessions in the Pacific. Australia and New Zealand were much alarmed. The former wished to annex New Guinea and the latter was eager to forestall German penetration in the Samoan Islands. Their anxieties were not regarded favorably in Whitehall. In the great game of world politics, Pacific islands were minor pawns. The Germans secured control of Samoa and the scattered islands now held by the Japanese, as well as part of New

Guinea. Australia made good its claim to the southern part of that island and, after federation in 1900, began there an experiment in colonial tutelage that was to shed luster on the name of the great administrator, Sir Hubert Murray.

As long as they remained colonies, self-governing at home but powerless abroad, the Pacific Dominions had no option but to watch with growing fear the extension of German power in the Pacific. Not until the Boer War at the turn of the century did their potential force become obvious. The contingents they sent to South Africa strengthened their influence. Colonial conferences henceforth became imperial conferences. The colonies increasingly developed their new Dominion status, and when the First World War broke out they were ready to act not as dependents but as partners.

They acted very promptly to mop up the German possessions in the Pacific. New Zealand added Samoa to its long list of island dependencies. Australia took over German New Guinea and the adjacent islands. Expeditionary forces—the Anzacs—went to the Middle East and later to Western Europe.

Meantime, however, Japan had risen to power in the northeast. In the First World War, Japan was allied with Britain and her navy escorted many contingents of Australian and New Zealand troops across the Pacific and Indian oceans. But at the close of the war the growing power of Japan was felt to be an increasing menace. The official attitude, particularly of Australia, was not hostile to Japan and there is evidence that the renunciation of the Anglo-Japanese Alliance in 1921 did not represent Australian and New Zealand views, but rather was the result of American and Canadian insistence. The German islands north of the equator had been granted to Japan under League mandate by a compromise settlement in which Australia also received mandates in New Guinea, including New Britain, and New Zealand received a mandate for part of Samoa.

It was only when the furtive designs of Japan became clearer in her policy toward China and in the secrecy which masked the fortification of her newly acquired mandate that latent suspicion hardened into positive fear of Japan. Even then, the Dominions continued to rely upon the protection to be afforded by the Singapore base. It was New Zealand's stiff refusal to allow the League Secretariat to inspect conditions in Samoa which gave Japan a precedent in refusing similar inspection of her mandated islands. All through the 1920's, Australia continued to cultivate her economic and political relations with Japan. After the aggression at Mukden in September, 1931, there was more hesitancy; but the wool trade was profitable and appeasement continued. It was not until the attack on Shanghai that New Zealand took an open stand on the League Council and later at the Brussels Conference against Japan's policy. In doing so the new Labor government played an independent role and was not supported either by Britain or by Australia. There was much division of opinion in Australia, but the government in power held firm to the support of British diplomacy. Not until Pearl Harbor, when the full extent of Japan's designs were revealed, did it yield to popular pressure.

The lesson, however, has been bitter and has been thoroughly learned. The fall of Singapore, the capture of Australian troops there, and the succession of defeats that brought the enemy to the very door of Australia provide ample justification for a resurgent nationalism. After this war, Australia and New Zealand will place security first. They yielded after the last war to diplomacy which compromised and gave Japan outposts from which to prepare her Pacific campaign. But they will not agree to such a compromise after this war.

Side by side with Americans, and under the command of an American leader, they are now painfully winning their way back island by island and airfield by airfield across the conquered lands. Their soldiers, sailors, and airmen have fallen in such numbers that they are bound to demand that this tragedy shall not occur again. Their preference is for an international solution to the problem of security. They will undoubtedly claim the right to administer much of the territory that lies at the door, and they have proved in Papua their worthiness to act as trustees for the primitive island peoples. They will demand that the Japanese bases pass into friendly hands so that their menace will be removed.

But territorial possession of scattered atolls will not give security. The wars which threaten their security are world wars. In their own right and as members of the Commonwealth, they will work for collective security against aggression wherever it may occur. And they await with confident expectation the decision of the United States to become a main pillar of that security, so that not only in the Pacific, but the wide world over, men may live their lives in freedom from the fear of aggressive war.